Classical music

A concise history

Julian Rushton

Classical music

A concise history
from Gluck to Beethoven

with 50 illustrations

 Thames and Hudson

For my mother

Printed in Great Britain by
B.A.S. Printers Limited,
Over Wallop, Hampshire
Bound in Great Britain by
Bath Press, Bath

Contents

Preface

A full historical study of 'Classical' Music which adequately assessed its social and historical context, as well as paying due attention to the music itself, would occupy several volumes. In covering the period from roughly the mid-eighteenth century to 1830 I have endeavoured to show the main changes in music and musical life, as well as the continuum of musical styles. Some of what I cover might be considered 'Baroque', and some is certainly considered 'Romantic'. No apology is needed for any overlap between this *History* and those which precede and follow it in the series currently in preparation. There are no complete breaks in the continuum and to pretend otherwise by rigidly partitioning off volumes from each other would be to falsify history.

While references to contemporary authors may be fully clear from the text – which is free of footnotes – certain quoted authors are included in the Select bibliography, where the reader is pointed, in most cases, to an English translation; any translations not so acknowledged are my own. I have otherwise included a short bibliography of works treating the period in general, documentary studies, and a selection of biographical studies. For fuller bibliographies the reader is directed to the appropriate volumes of *The New Oxford History of Music* (see Abraham and Wellesz) or to *The New Grove* (see Sadie).

I would like to thank the staff of Thames and Hudson for their patience; numerous colleagues and students for their ideas, and for listening to mine; and particularly Arnold Whittall, for allowing me to see a draft of the opening sections of his *Romantic Music: A Concise History*.

JULIAN RUSHTON
Leeds 1985

1 *The Apotheosis of Homer* (1778); plaque by John Flaxman expressing the ideals of 'noble simplicity and calm grandeur' praised in antiquity by Winckelmann and emulated by Gluck (see chapter 3).

CHAPTER ONE

Introduction
Classicism and its background

The epithet 'Classical' is nowadays indiscriminately applied to almost any Western music that is not jazz, folk, or popular. It has various connotations within musical criticism, of varying precision, but the standard literary and art-historical sense is not among them. Admittedly we speak of musical 'Classics', works of established greatness, but in so doing we are not referring even indirectly to the music of 'Classical' civilizations as a stylistic model or standard of excellence. Reference to the ancient world suggests Humanism, or Neoclassicism, one among many significant ideals of the late eighteenth century. But the title of this history refers to a degeneration of 'Classical' into a chronological term, covering the period roughly from the middle of the eighteenth century to the death of Beethoven.

'Classical' in this sense suggests the antithesis 'Romantic'. But while many composers of the nineteenth century actually regarded themselves as Romantic, there is no reason to suppose that even the most culturally aware of eighteenth-century composers considered themselves 'Classical', nor did they believe that they were writing 'Classics'. With few exceptions – Gluck's last operas, Haydn's oratorios, the later works of Beethoven – composers of this era wrote for their own day and expected their music to become quickly outdated. Nevertheless our secular musical life has long depended upon music written between about 1770 and 1830. While the best of this music has no doubt suffered misunderstanding, performing malpractice, and periods of neglect, it has never been forgotten. Music revived from earlier periods is measured against the continued presence in our musical consciousness of those whom we call the 'Viennese Classics'; while the shadow of Beethoven, who is also claimed by Romanticism, lay so deeply across his successors that their orientation is partly determined by an unprecedented sense of inferiority. We have, therefore, because of the way its immediate posterity saw this music, the formation of a secular canon of works of artistic authority; the circumstance in which, as Kermode observes, the question 'What is a Classic?' needs to be asked. The first identified Classics of Western music are the fruits ripened in the Classical period: overture, solo concerto, symphony; string quartet, sonata; the operas of Mozart, the songs of Schubert.

In the late eighteenth century, for the first time in the Christian era, secular music completely outstrips sacred music in importance. The masses and oratorios of Haydn and Beethoven are pinnacles of musical form, not contributions to a liturgy. The religious revival so important to Romanticism is in part a reaction against the secular values of eighteenth-century society and philosophy – values which coincided with the establishment of the secular canon of symphonies, quartets, choral works, even oratorios designed for the concert-hall and singing a religion of humanity rather than of any established Church. Romanticism, however, is also deeply indebted to the French Revolution, which in turn was the realization of ideas articulated in mid-eighteenth-century philosophical and political thought. In the arts, Romanticism is self-consciously built upon the achievements of the eighteenth century, and especially so in music, where composers worked to continue a line of Classics which they augmented by the discovery of greatness in a more distant past, notably J. S. Bach.

'Classical', therefore, originates in an enduring recognition of the value of certain musical works, rather than in qualities peculiar to those works. The implication of Classical as opposed to Romantic is often taken to be a tendency towards formal discipline rather than strength of feeling. The aestheticians and educationalists of music in the late eighteenth century, on the contrary, emphasized feeling rather than form; and it was the age of Romanticism which showed so marked an interest in structure. It would be wrong to suppose that Classical music is not replete with feeling. What academics later classified as typical forms of the period, and as models of balanced structure, were novel for the composers who used them. They should be heard not as forms but as processes; they were never structural moulds into which musical ideas might be poured. Thus Joseph Haydn is often considered remarkably free in his structures, whereas in fact he was free in invention of forms and rigorous in application of general principles. When the music was no longer new, it became a standard of excellence, and it was natural for pedagogues to study it for procedures to emulate. Academic criticism has too often imposed on the practice of the eighteenth century ideas which had their origin only later. In order to view the Classical era, we need to take off our nineteenth-century spectacles. An objective more characteristic of our own time, impossible to achieve but rewarding to pursue, is to view an earlier age as it saw itself.

Like the Athens of Sophocles, which was also that of Thucydides, late eighteenth-century Europe was the setting both of artistic grandeur and of political change marked by violence. The age of Mozart and Beethoven opened amid dynastic fighting and included the bloodiest revolution before the twentieth century, followed inevitably by reaction. The age of Enlightenment and reform was also an age of autocracy, of Frederick the Great and Maria Theresia; the age of Revolution led to repression, to Napoleon and Metternich.

The majority of musicians were employees from the servant or lower middle classes, and suffered from inefficient management over which they had no control. They also lacked security, as is clear from Dittersdorf's memoirs; for a prince, as for a modern branch of government, dismissing musicians was a simple economy. Musicians were poorly paid, even with occasional perquisites, and payment could be arbitrarily withheld without explanation or redress. Nevertheless opportunities were growing for them to avoid the constraints and indignities of court and church employment, and to develop an independent subsistence. Municipal and republican employment, though scarcely better paid, was more secure; the work was just as hard but the artist was able to exert some control over it, and petitions to authority did not need to be couched in terms of sickening obsequiousness. More important still, the capital cities of monarchies, especially Paris and London, were developing a middle-class market for music, in response to which musicians made themselves entrepreneurs as well as composers and performers, and thus joined the same social class as most of their customers.

The altered status of musicians resulted from gradual change, not from revolution. Even today musicians may be employed by a church or secular authority, and the composer's place in society is less clear than it was when he had specific duties. Freelance activity is still precarious; in the eighteenth century, as Mozart found, it was perilous even for a genius. The freelance had to compete with musicians in established posts who supplemented their income by taking private pupils. If compositions were sold it was once for all, with no benefit from royalties or performing rights. The opera composer was paid if he directed productions in various centres, but travel undermined security of income from teaching at home. The sale of music, however, was a developing asset, both in printed form and in authorized manuscript copies. Keyboard playing and solo singing were social accomplishments, and the emergent middle classes also provided a market for chamber and orchestral music in separate instrumental parts (many works survive only in this form so that the modern scholar has to reconstruct the score). The musical amateur also paid to hear the professional, and the travelling instrumentalist took his place beside the opera singer among the better paid. The virtuoso may still have been regarded in Liszt's day as a tradesman, but he was no longer a servant, and he could ply his trade for profit.

Such conditions assisted the development of new genres for the amateur and the virtuoso – the short piano piece, the study, the pot-pourri – as well as new interpretations of old procedures such as fantasia and variations. A gap appeared between lightweight and serious genres. Among the latter the symphony has pride of place in the public mind, but symphonic essence is also to be found in chamber music, the solo sonata, and the concerto. Social conditions encouraged the marketing of serious genres in the late eighteenth century, and their establishment in the concert life of the nineteenth. This last development coincides with a new kind of appreciation of instrumental music. It is evident, however, that social, political, and economic forces cannot account for the highest development of these forms, and stand to the birth of high Classical and Romantic music as a midwife rather than a parent.

The period from about 1750 to 1900, at the centre of which so many social factors changed musicians' lives, may still be considered a single unit in the history of Western music. From Classical to Romantic music, as Blume argues, must be seen as a shift of emphasis rather than a radical reorientation of the elements of musical discourse. The 'Classical' and 'Romantic' volumes in the present history, therefore, are not separated by any gulf in the handling of the elements of music: pitch, rhythm, counterpoint, harmony, timbre, structural processes. In discussing the mid-eighteenth century, it is reasonable to think in terms of a stylistic reorientation, so that certain long-lived composers – notably Telemann, and in a later generation C. P. E. Bach – may be said to belong both to Baroque and Classical music. There is really no such progressive reorientation in the major composers who seem to straddle the Classic–Romantic divide; the 'Classic' and 'Romantic' in Beethoven, Schubert, Rossini or Weber coexist and complement each other. Apparent inconsistencies in a composer's style are usually explicable as the product of artistic intention, of genre, or simply of market forces. The musician was a different social animal by 1830, and the possibilities of the art itself for communication to new audiences – and their relation to the composer *as* audiences rather than as patrons or congregations – had already undergone a major alteration, one which reached a significant stage in the mature symphonic music of Joseph Haydn. At the outset of our period the public world of secular music was dominated by Italian opera; at the end, although the latter continued to flourish, the summit of musical achievement seems in retrospect, and seemed to many people at the time, to be instrumental music of symphonic scope.

The intellectual temper of the mid-eighteenth century has led to its appellation 'the Age of Enlightenment'. This was not religious enlightenment but on the contrary a secular awakening, following the astronomical and physical discoveries of Galileo and Newton. Despite the maintenance of religious observance, the churches' control over intellectual developments, already weakened since the Reformation, became merely a stimulus to thought which defied dogma. For the intellectual, exile, in which thought was free and very often reached publication, replaced imprisonment or death; Switzerland became a haven for Voltaire and Jean-Jacques Rousseau although their main sphere of influence was still Paris. The Enlightenment is epitomized in the *Encyclopédie* of Diderot and d'Alembert, published in twenty-eight volumes from 1751 to 1772; many musical articles were contributed by Rousseau. Its aim was no less than to encompass the sum of human knowledge. That such a task was conceivable, and eagerly embraced, is an indication less of the limits of eighteenth-century science than of the inspired ambitions of rationalist philosophy.

Besides wishing to classify knowledge, the *philosophes* believed in the perfectibility of human society. As a condition of freedom, they looked to political and social reform. Such doctrines were evidently subversive of the political order, in which monarchical government still prevailed and England, whose monarchy was the most nearly constitutional, had most recently suffered revolutions. The pattern of European government was the ruthlessly centralized autocracy of Louis XIV of France, symbolized by the grandeur of his palace, the folly of his wars and the expense of his opera. Even if they were not the administrative centres of empires, imitations of Versailles sprang up everywhere, including Esterház, where Haydn worked in the establishment of an enormously wealthy prince subservient to the Imperial government of Vienna, and Sanssouci, whence Frederick II laid the foundations of modern Germany by expanding the power and influence of Prussia. Frederick, in rivalling Louis XIV's successors, saw in himself an alternative model: the ideal governor, Plato's enlightened despot, gathering round him not only distinguished artists and musicians but thinkers, even subversives like Voltaire.

In an age of dynastic government, linguistic and ethnic units were slow to develop national consciousness. The unification of Italy and Germany did not occur until late in the next century. Eighteenth-century Germany consisted of innumerable princedoms and some free cities, Italy of independent republics (notably Venice), semi-

2 Palace of Nikolaus I at Esterház (1766). The view from the air shows the grandeur and severity of design for both palace and garden.

independent princedoms, areas under foreign domination, and Papal lands. The Holy Roman Empire survived until its overthrow by Napoleon, but was an anachronism; the elective Emperor was invariably the head of the Hapsburgs and hereditary ruler of Austria, controlling Hungary, Bohemia, and an empire growing with the receding tide of Turkish power. The War of the Austrian Succession (1741–5) was caused by the heritage falling to a woman, the formidable Maria Theresia, sometimes considered the model for Mozart's Queen of Night. For many years she ruled jointly with her son, who in 1780 ascended the throne as Joseph II. Joseph attempted reforms which brought Austria nearer than Prussia to the main stream of Enlightenment; the Holy Roman Emperor was prepared to tolerate the Freemasons. Joseph, however, attempted too much too quickly. Even before the French revolutionary threat, but in face of renewed Turkish wars, he moved to suppress the fermentation of ideas; and his successors established something like a police state, whose capital was the home of Beethoven and Schubert.

Whatever the economic causes of the French revolution, the remoteness of Versailles from intellectual exploration cannot be discounted as a factor in generating violence. Paris itself was a cosmopolitan city, in which the intellectual, if not the fashionable, tone was set by the middle class. The hope of aggrandizement at the expense of an old enemy made the French government support the American revolution; George III appeared more of a tyrant to America than to London, and in consequence American intellectuals such as Benjamin Franklin naturally turned to the enlightened thought of Paris. In the constitution of the United States, European liberals could see many of their ideals embodied, and it was perhaps the single most hopeful sign of the development of human society along rationalist lines, as well as being symptomatic of the wider horizons which now began to be revealed to many people of relatively humble origins.

As an age of scientific advance and the classification of knowledge, the Enlightenment gave rise to copious writings on music. Publications on theory continued a long-standing preoccupation of musical intellectuals; manuals of instruction in performance and composition appeared with increasing frequency; and the late eighteenth century saw the beginnings of modern musical historiography.

The *Encyclopédie* itself was classified 'by order of subjects' and revised, the *Encyclopédie méthodique (Musique)* appearing in two widely-spaced volumes (1791 and 1818), the latter largely the work of an early proponent of music analysis, J. J. de Momigny. One feature of these volumes was that they reprinted, and then disputed with, articles in Rousseau's remarkable *Dictionnaire de la musique* (1767), a work which is a perfect example of how even the Enlightenment did not feel it necessary to disentangle scholarship from opinionated criticism. The Encyclopaedists were advocates of modern (Italian) music; and there developed a conflict between those who believed in the growing perfection of music and its degeneracy. The latter view was espoused by Sir John Hawkins (*A General History of the Science and Practice of Music*, 1776); the view that British music was ruined by Handel still has some sympathizers. Charles Burney, on the other hand, researched as an antiquarian who found in the past only proof of the superiority of the present. In his *A General History of Music* (four volumes, 1776–89), the energetic consultation of continental sources detailed in his delightful travel books does not prevent disproportionate space being allocated to Italian opera in England. A more dispassionate account of the Middle Ages appears in J. B. de la Borde's massive *Essai sur la musique ancienne et moderne* (1780). The greatest scholar of the age, Padre Martini, friend and counterpoint teacher to Johann Christian Bach and Mozart, still had not reached the Middle Ages in the three extant volumes of his *Storia della musica* (1761–81).

The major theoretical controversy, centred in Berlin, was between the admirers of Rameau's harmonic system and those who favoured traditional instruction by counterpoint and figured bass. Marpurg, who rose to be director of the Prussian State Lottery, wrote a 'Critical Introduction' to music history (1759) and a textbook on fugue (1753); his advocacy of Rameau was disputed by pupils of J. S. Bach such as Kirnberger, Agricola, and Carl Philipp Emanuel Bach. The power of J. S. Bach's influence as a teacher and example should not be forgotten; his 48 Preludes and Fugues were widely studied in manuscript copies and were published well before the 'Bach revival' associated with Mendelssohn, which was based upon the rediscovery of his choral music. Forkel's biography of Bach was written as early as 1802, on a rising tide of nationalism; Bach was a model of German virtues needed for the recovery of greatness in the face of the post-Revolutionary French empire.

The spirit of Enlightenment is more truly represented by internationalism. In his *Versuch* (*Essay on the True Art of Playing the Keyboard*), C. P. E. Bach extols the musical virtues of the French keyboard school and Italian opera, without disloyalty to the German tradition of which he always considered his father the supreme representative. This fascinating book combines instruction in dexterity and taste with improvisational, and hence compositional, suggestions still used today to counter the Rameau school of harmonic thought. Appearing in 1753, the *Versuch* is contemporary with tutors by Quantz for the flute and Leopold Mozart for the violin; it is one of the headaches of modern reconstruction of historic performing style that these three authoritative texts are not entirely compatible. The *Versuch* is also an aesthetic document of importance, which had its effect in the musical sections (by Kirnberger and Schulz) of Sulzer's *General Theory of the Fine Arts* (Berlin, 1771–4). Bach is also the major model for subsequent keyboard tutors, by Türk, Milchmeyer and Adam, the latter forming part of a series commissioned by the newly-established Paris Conservatoire around the turn of the century. Another major theorist was Koch, who laid down the principles of *galant* composition in *Versuch einer Einleitung zur Composition* (1782–93); he also produced an important lexicon of musical terms (1802). Koch influenced Beethoven's friend Antonín Reicha (1770–1836), who taught at the Paris Conservatoire and produced a series of treatises between 1814 and 1833 on melody, counterpoint and harmony (including a novel section on instrumentation), composition, and dramatic composition. Beethoven's pupil Karl Czerny (1791–1857) translated Reicha's books and produced his own treatises on piano playing (with immense quantities of technical material for which he is still remembered), extemporization and composition. Even when Romanticism tended towards comprehensive artistic theories in which music played a leading part, music maintained its own historical, critical, theoretical, analytical and instructional literature, whose value for our understanding of how composers may have thought is only now being appreciated.

Although the history of musical life can only be fully understood as part of political and social history, the history of music itself is more tenuously connected even with the other arts. The arts do not work in phase. A great age for music does not necessarily coincide with greatness in the visual arts or literature; 'Viennese Classical' music was not the contemporary of equally great visual art, while the finest literature of the time is generally considered Romantic. Nor were the nations of Europe in phase; in this period, Germany and Britain may have pride of place in literature, Britain and France in the visual arts, but Germany, Austria, Italy and France in music. Connections between politics, philosophy and the arts, and among the arts, are seldom straightforward, nor do they necessarily have much importance for the understanding of musical works. In retrospect the vision of a better future for mankind in charge of its own destiny finds a belated artistic consummation, in a period of renewed despotism, in the music of Beethoven. Most obviously this spirit affects his Ninth Symphony, with its ode to joy (a codeword for freedom). In general, however, music developed on its own terms, especially when it functioned not only as entertainment or as support for a text, but as a mode of refined discourse which transcends words and normal existence with them. Music such as Beethoven's late quartets is as impervious to political, social or historical interpretation as it is to explanation by reference to other arts.

It is true that Haydn dressed up a petition on behalf of musicians in need of a holiday in a symphony (no. 45, the *Farewell*). Did he distrust verbal petitions, or doubt their efficacy? Certainly Nikolaus I Esterházy understood the message, and Haydn won his point. If music partakes of a political attitude, it is usually through attachment to words. The period we are considering saw the emergence of nation states and their national anthems. *God save the King* crystallized after 1745, when two of the most popular tunes were *Rule, Britannia* and *Roast Beef of Old England*. The French revolution spawned, among many other songs, the *Marseillaise*, to which Haydn's great hymn 'Gott erhalte Franz den Kaiser' was a loyal response. Yet the sentiment of the words hardly affects the absolute musician who took such themes for variation (Haydn in his *Emperor* quartet or Beethoven in piano variations on *God Save the King* and *Rule, Britannia*).

A political message is, however, a quality of some of the greatest music dramas of the time. Mozart made Beaumarchais' *Le mariage de Figaro* into an opera when it was forbidden in the spoken theatre of Vienna, and he included in the first finale of *Don Giovanni* a setting of the words 'Long live liberty' inflated far beyond the requirements of the drama. It is perhaps significant that these lines were missing from

3 'Gott erhalte Franz den Keiser', Haydn's Imperial Hymn (headed 'Folksong'), set for voices and orchestra (1797).

the libretto submitted to the censor in advance of the performance. In *The Magic Flute* Mozart, or his librettist, extols the virtues of enlightened government by an elected ruler; moreover the Orator voices a doubt as to whether Tamino, being a prince, can survive the ordeals. Sarastro replies that he is more than a Prince; he is a man. Beethoven's *Fidelio* ends with a hymn to Freedom more explicit than that of the Ninth Symphony.

In *The Magic Flute* Tamino finds himself before three temples (ill. 22). Rejected by Nature and Reason, he is greeted by Wisdom; without knowledge of who is enlightened (Sarastro) and who evil (the Queen), he cannot proceed to comprehend Reason, the proper exercise of wisdom in thought and judgment, or Nature, the understanding of natural law and, by extension, the rights of living beings. 'Man is born free, and is everywhere in chains': Rousseau's dictum is exaggerated – many were born into slavery and many free minds exercised their freedom – but it touched a chord in the Enlightenment, as did his concept of the 'noble savage', natural man uncorrupted by civilization, although in fact the life of this paragon was usually nasty, brutish and short. Reasonableness, naturalness, became criteria for the judgment of art: their enemy complexity, contrivance. Striving for simplicity and directness was fundamental to the evolution of musical language in the mid-eighteenth century.

Such striving is not, however, a defining element in the best of what followed. On the basis of a new simplicity musicians built a new complexity. Directness of utterance becomes one possibility, to be selected as appropriate. The language of music has seldom been so rich, especially once the techniques of an earlier era had been reabsorbed; the styles of the Baroque fertilized the Classical style, just as the styles of the Renaissance had entered the Baroque after a period in which complexity was rejected. *The Magic Flute* is a repository of almost every available style; its simple movements are like strophic folksong, its most complex arias approach the idiom of *opera seria*, and the music for the enlightened priesthood ranges from hymnlike purity to a chorale woven about with Bachian counterpoint. A similar synthesis of artlessness and contrivance informs Beethoven's Ninth, which in this respect – notwithstanding a common nineteenth-century view of it – is the culmination of its era, not a pattern for the next.

The formation of stylistic tendencies characteristic of the mid-eighteenth century preceded any substantial change in society or in the social position of musicians. The mid-century style is not easy to define today, when we are more familiar with what preceded and followed it. One term used for the mid-century is 'pre-Classical', but this accords its music (including late Telemann, Gluck and early Haydn) an undeservedly provisional status. The art-historical term 'Rococo' is applied by Lowinsky to the mid-century and even the Mozart period, for which it seems inappropriately decorative. In its more common usage, as a localized development of Baroque, Rococo is better suited to early eighteenth-century French composers, such as Couperin.

The term which at the time would have been recognized as virtually synonymous with 'modern' is *'galant* style'. This too may appear to suggest prettiness and insubstantiality, but it usefully distinguishes the up-to-date idiom from the strict styles which were still cultivated, and not only in church music. The new style arose concurrently with the development of a more sophisticated mode of

4 Neo-Palladian grandeur in rural Suffolk: the rotunda at Ickworth begun by Frederick Hervey, 4th Earl of Bristol and Bishop of Derry, in 1795.

Italian comic opera, and appears in instrumental music well before 1750. There was no seismic upheaval to compare with the invention of monody 150 years before, or the weakening of tonality to the point of extinction 150 years later. Most composers adapted themselves, in some degree, to the new style; in this respect J. S. Bach's continued cultivation of traditional values, in such late masterpieces as *The Art of Fugue*, was exceptional. In the next generation, C. P. E. Bach, educated by his father but knowing the daring music of Domenico Scarlatti, produced church music associated with older styles and keyboard works whose effect is felt as late as Beethoven.

What perhaps most distinguished the mid-century idiom is that it was almost entirely international. The national styles of the late Baroque broke down with the *style galant* into an idiom which, while able to accommodate national traits (no Italian would compose like C. P. E. Bach or Grétry), was increasingly founded in common practices. Internationalism was deliberately cultivated; musicians,

5 One-manual harpsichord by Pascal Taskin (Paris, 1786), lacquered with elegant *chinoiserie*.

who have seldom been so mobile as in this period, could practise their art in remote places without much change of style. Even in France, where the serious opera remained fiercely nationalistic until the 1770s, the common style prevailed in instrumental music. Such a widespread consensus, with different areas displaying regional accents of a common tongue, is characteristic of the Enlightenment, in which scientific ideas and philosophies were transmitted and developed internationally.

Internationalism also prevailed in other arts; literature was extensively translated and two of the most successful Italian comic operas of the day were based on an English epistolary novel (Piccinni's *La Cecchina*, on Richardson's *Pamela*) and a French play (Paisiello's *Il barbiere di Siviglia*, after Beaumarchais). Artists and decorators from Italy practised as widely as Italian musicians, and Italy continued to dominate stage design, at least until 1800. Also international were fashions, such as that for the exotic; operatic

22

subjects ranged from China to Peru. Yet so ingrained was the musical *lingua franca*, the expressiveness and brilliance of the *galant* style, that music itself resisted exotic influence. 'Turkish music', the percussion group of drum, triangle, and cymbal, entered the orchestra (Gluck, *La rencontre imprévue* (1764) and *Iphigénie en Tauride* (1779); Mozart, *Die Entführung* (1782); Haydn, *Military* Symphony, no. 100). Otherwise exoticism was visual; chinoiserie was for the decorator, not the musician.

Neither '*galant*' nor 'Classical' implies coolness. Contemporary Neoclassicism embodied strong, if idealized, feeling, and in the painting of J. L. David anticipated and later symbolized the heroic aspect of the French Revolution. If Neoclassicism is applicable to music, it is in the revival of the values of humanistic opera, and among its aims was the depiction of extreme emotional states, for which Gluck was at times severely criticized. Contemporary with Gluck's Neoclassical operas was a short-lived but significant literary movement in Germany, known as *Sturm und Drang* (storm and stress) after a play by Klinger (1776) set in revolutionary America. In marked contrast to Neoclassical drama, which preserved the forms of the French seventeenth century, this movement took the plays of Shakespeare as its model, both for their freedom of form and their vehemence of expression. Friedrich Schiller (1759–1805) cultivated Shakespeare's form and spirit in a study of an outlaw, *Die Räuber*; he later turned to huge battle-filled canvasses (*Wilhelm Tell*) and dynastic and nationalistic intrigue (*Don Carlos*), as well as more intimate tragedy (*Kabale und Liebe*). It was, again, not for fifty years that music could assimilate such passion. Despite Rossini's *Guillaume Tell* (1829), the true operatic counterpart of Schiller is Verdi. The dominating literary figure of the age, Johann Wolfgang Goethe (1749–1832), participated in *Sturm und Drang* in his novel of middle-class tragedy, the semi-autobiographical *Sorrows of the young Werther* (1774). Suicides in imitation of Goethe's hero anticipated the world-weariness of the next century's young Romantics. Goethe, however, also cultivated Neoclassicism; his *Iphigenie auf Tauris* (begun in 1779) is coincidentally contemporary to Gluck's opera on the same subject.

In France, modern drama took a domestic, novel-like form. Denis Diderot (1713–84) was not only the leading spirit of the great *Encyclopédie* and a stimulating writer on music; he affected a generation with his 'tearful drama' (*comédie larmoyante*) *Le fils naturel*

6 *Sturm und Drang: Avalanche* (1803) by the Alsatian P. de Loutherberg, who was also a theatre designer, depicts human terror in the face of natural catastrophe.

(*The Bastard Son*, 1757). Assisted by the cult of the English novel (Richardson, Fielding, Smollett), the impact on French opera was immediate. Beaumarchais (1732–99) revived the spirit of Molière, disguising political thrust beneath ingenious farce; his *Figaro* plays conformed perfectly to expectation when adapted for *opera buffa*. In the same period, amid the literary life of London which viewed opera with suspicion, David Garrick (1717–79) brought about a regeneration of histrionic art. He excelled in Shakespeare, but his influence was felt on the Neoclassical dramatic forms, the action ballet and Gluckian opera.

In so richly diverse a period, generalizations about artistic tendencies hold no water. But it is important to recognize the difference between the effects of other artistic movements on the uses to which music is put, and their effect on the language of music itself.

The first is of major importance, but of necessity appears as much in extraneous matter, such as opera libretti, as in music itself. The second is more difficult to assess with confidence. The term *Sturm und Drang* is used to describe a short period in the output of several composers, principally Haydn in the early 1770s. But it must be emphasized that the most concentrated period of musical storm and stress *preceded* the literary movement; and that the musical phenomenon was primarily Austrian, whereas the literature was from north Germany. There is really no connection between these two 'movements', and use of the literary term for music, with the authority of Brook and Ratner, is potentially confusing.

On the other hand, cultivation of the 'tearful' or pathetic is exactly paralleled by elements in the *galant* style which contemporary critics might have called 'sentimental': meaning, as in Sterne's *A Sentimental Journey*, the cultivation of genuine feeling. Highly wrought yet directly expressive music embodying the subtlest shifts of feeling, such as is found in C. P. E. Bach's keyboard sonatas and Haydn's early slow movements, is called the style of 'sensibility' (*Empfindsamkeit*). It is calculated to appeal to complex feelings, without being complicated musically by 'learned' counterpoint; much of its effectiveness resides in intricate ornamentation which does not disguise clear, affecting melody (and in Bach, searching harmony). Such music appealed strongly to the new consumers, who were not much interested in the sublimities of the semi-divine heroes of serious opera. Transmuted by an elaborated musical technique, the *galant* and 'sentimental' reach their apogee in the slow movement of Beethoven's Ninth Symphony, shortly before the composer, through Schiller's Ode, embraced humanity.

CHAPTER TWO

Italian opera and the early symphony

Jean-François Marmontel, an ardent champion of Piccinni against Gluck, dated the inception of 'modern' music to the point 'when *Vinci* for the first time plotted the curve of periodic song. . . . It was then that the great mystery of melody was revealed' (*Essai*, 1777). Leonardo Vinci (*c.* 1690 or 1696–1730) composed two dozen serious operas as well as several comedies in Neapolitan dialect. His importance was widely recognized, even by those with no axe to grind; Burney's *History* states that he simplified and polished melody and directed attention to the vocal line 'by disentangling it from fugue, complication, and laboured contrivance'. Vinci was admired by Metastasio (1698–1782), the reformer who established the pattern of serious Italian opera libretti for the rest of the century, and by Handel, who used his music in the *pasticcii* (operas confected out of older operas) with which he filled his seasons in London. Vinci paved the way for his better-known but even shorter-lived pupil Giovanni Battista Pergolesi (1710–1736), who fed the mainstream of European

7 Caricature of Leonardo Vinci by P. L. Ghezzi, showing the composer directing a performance with rolled-up music paper.

opera through a handful of outstandingly successful works using, in comedy, an internationally acceptable Italian. Pergolesi's post-humous fame was legendary; much music was misattributed to him, since anything bearing his name would sell (this was later to happen with Haydn, in his lifetime). If Vinci was the leading spirit of a new 'Neapolitan' style which was to conquer Europe, Pergolesi became symbolic of its liveliness, its pathos, its delicacy and youthfulness.

Needless to say, the *galant* style did not spring into life fully formed in Naples, nor did Vinci invent melody. To a modern ear his music sounds closer to the late Baroque than to the Classical style. It is, however, a misunderstanding of musical processes to assume any clean break between Baroque and Classical; such a break only appears if we compare the maturest developments of each. Continuity of idiom from the early to the late eighteenth century was maintained through the continuing appeal of composers of Vinci's generation, such as Domenico Scarlatti (1685–1757) and Johann Adolph Hasse (1699–1783). The Baroque style, as the career of Telemann shows, was undermined from within. The new style shows continuity with the past in its use of striking motifs spun out by sequential development, and in its lively figuration, reminiscent of Vivaldi's generation. It anticipates later developments in its dependence on periodic cadences and its extension of material by opposition and symmetry. It is not surprising that in retrospect, the mid-century style appears transitional. In reality, however, no period is merely a transition (or every period is transitional). It is false to view the early eighteenth century as a period of stability, the 'age of Bach and Handel'. If we accept the over-simplification that these masters represent a plateau in stylistic development, the fields around them remained fertile with new ideas and ways of presenting them. The same, at the end of our period, is true of the 'Age of Beethoven'.

The music of the mid-eighteenth century is lively and various, and if it lacks the intellectual gravity of the ripest Baroque and Classical styles, it has numerous attractions peculiar to itself, manifested in opera, keyboard music, and symphony. The source of most of its vitality is Italian comic opera. To put across a comic plot, in which two or more characters must often sing with opposed sentiments, demands a flexible style with a relatively simple basis. 'High Baroque' music is texturally controlled by the strong reciprocal relationship of a treble and bass of almost equal melodic interest. The continuo element was usually improvised, on a keyboard or plucked and fretted stringed instrument such as the lute; it realized the chordal (vertical) implications of essentially polyphonic (horizontal) musical thought in accordance with a well-understood code. In every genre, Baroque music worked by extension, spinning out and sequentially reproducing units in a seamless web; each movement was thus strongly unified in sentiment. This style is more suited to solemnity, grandeur and pathos than to the cut and thrust of naturalistic comedy.

Theorists identified the main ingredient of the new musical style as the melodic 'period', and valued symmetry for the clear presentation of an expressive idea. The *galant* style accordingly emphasizes the often ornate treble, and its supporting bass is decidedly subservient. The harmonies continue to be filled in, and periodic cadences defined, by the continuo. (The practice of directing performances from the keyboard remained at least until the end of the century, although by then musical textures were complete without it). Treble-dominated texture was matched by periodicity of phrase; instead of a seamless web, moving swiftly and easily between tonal centres closely related to the principal key of the piece, the mid-century style marks each tonal stage in the evolution of a movement by decisive cadential

8 'Ach, ich fühl's': Pamina's aria, the moment of highest pathos in *The Magic Flute*; autograph (1791).

punctuation. In consequence, the temporary establishment of an alternative tonal centre acquires dramatic potential, and the simplest key-relations eventually became capable of supporting enormous lengths of music.

The *galant* style is not frivolous; an example of deep pathos, whose opening, at least, is compatible with the style of sixty years before, is Mozart's aria 'Ach, ich fühl's' from *The Magic Flute* (1791). As the piece develops, the symmetry of *galant* music and its harmonic lucidity are compromised by asymmetrical phrases and the subtle infiltration of chromatic harmonies. The complexity of the Classical style is partly the result of its historical consciousness, its assimilation of those styles against which the *galant* was in revolt, but it is far more the result of searching for expressive range and architectural span. It would be too much to pretend that there is an unbroken (still less an inevitable) progression from Pergolesi's comedies to Beethoven's symphonies. But the former affected the development of the symphony in its early stages, from which the symphonic form of Beethoven, if not its substance, ultimately derives.

Pergolesi's comic style is not essentially different from the *galant* parts of his religious music, or from his style in *opera seria*. It does, however, contain flashes of boldness and a precision of characterization which surpass his other works both musically and dramatically. It is no great distance from Serpetta, in *La serva padrona* (1733), to Mozart's Despina (*Così*, 1790), and the bass singer (virtually banished) from *opera seria*) is type-cast as the perplexed master Uberto. Yet Pergolesi's style emerged from the mingled comedy and sentiment of seventeenth-century opera, Stradella and A. Scarlatti. The scintillating duet 'Lo conosco a quegli occhietti' which ends the first intermezzo of *La serva padrona* was singled out by Rousseau as 'a model of pleasant song, of melodic unity, of simple, brilliant, and pure harmony, of declaimed dialogue . . .'.

This praise is well earned, but 'unity' demands explanation. What is most striking, and lends vigour and truth to the dialogue, is the *variety* of melodic shapes. Rousseau meant that clarity of phrasing imposes a larger pattern onto this variety, so ensuring a continuity of musical sense equivalent to unity. Besides being wonderfully comic, the cut and thrust of this duet begets a type of symphonic argument. Instruments too can be given characteristic musical ideas, and the element of competition (more explicit in a concerto) can be married to a consistency of overall direction governed by tonality.

Unity remained an important element in musical theory. Several authors, Rousseau among them, attacked Gluck for setting different sections of text not merely with a difference of mood, but in different tempi (as in Alceste's rondo, 'Non, ce n'est point un sacrifice'). 'Where is the unity? This is no aria, but a succession of several arias.' Dramatic situations did not license a breach of the enduring Baroque principle of unity of affection. Contrast should be contained within a single tempo; as the Italophile critic Framery put it in 1802, 'a periodic aria' should contain one affection, but 'if it contains several, they are in opposition, which forms a connection between them, and still constitutes a single idea'. If this was true of music in which the text justifies contrast, it was still more true of instrumental music where there is no text to provide an explanation for diversity, and variety has to be understood in musically self-sufficient terms. Unity is founded in an underlying sense of continuity bridging clearly articulated phrases, and in an increasing tendency, not always exemplified by Pergolesi, towards regular phrase-lengths. This underlying unity of rhythm and tonality makes surface variety of motifs and colour acceptable, and permits substantial contrasts within a single tempo, a conception not much used in earlier instrumental music but fundamental to that of the late eighteenth and nineteenth centuries.

It is widely recognized that eighteenth-century music, vocal and instrumental, owes much of its rhythmic character to the standard dance forms, and may even derive part of its meaning from the social contexts in which particular dances were used; the *locus classicus* is the first finale of Mozart's *Don Giovanni*, combining the aristocratic Minuet, the popular but increasingly urbanized Contredanse, and the rustic Ländler. Contemporary theorists recognized the origins of characteristic symphonic styles in these, and the March, Sarabande and Gavotte (see Ratner, *Classic Music*). But the vocal model was no less important to the development of a free and independent instrumental language. Operatic aria and ensemble showed how single ideas could be extended in a periodic musical structure (particularly the aria of sentiment, model of so many instrumental slow movements), or several ideas combined in a symphonic argument (particularly in the fast outer movements of quartets and symphonies).

Italian opera also provided a model for symphonic form in its overture, usually, indeed, called *sinfonia*. The overture to an Italian opera was a short symphony in three movements, a moderately fast opening, a slow centre, and either a very fast finale or a Minuet. This order and relative speed of movements was common in the Baroque concerto, also a significant model of motivic extension and development. But in the overture of mid-century Italian opera we have the symphony not in embryo but fully fledged; overtures could be translated to the concert room without incongruity, or a symphony could be used before an opera. This interchangeability of function continued as late as Haydn, J. C. Bach, and Mozart, whose Symphony no. 32 is an Italian overture of related type, a slow movement sandwiched between the outer parts of a single Allegro.

The first substantial symphonist had a French father and an Italian mother. Giovanni Battista Sammartini (*c.* 1700–1775) wrote only a few operas, and those early in his career; he held the post of *maestro di capella* in several Milan churches, by no means an unusual pluralism, and played a leading role in the musical life of Milan, under Austrian

9 Violin part headed 'Concerto/Overture' but in fact a late symphony by Sammartini (London, Bremner, 1766). The whole first movement is shown; note the frequent dynamic markings (*for*, loud; *po*, soft).

government from 1744 and the seat of a Hapsburg archduke. His early symphonies lie as close to the north Italian concerto (exemplified by Vivaldi) as to any operatic model. From about 1740 his music had fully assimilated the cut-and-thrust of *opera buffa* and the pathos of its slower music in the minor mode, while retaining the concerto's brilliance of string-writing. Sammartini's symphonies are serious works, yet not without humour; hence the Bohemian composer Josef Mysliveček (1737–81) declared Sammartini's style to be the origin of Haydn's. Haydn repudiated this, calling Sammartini a 'dauber', but there is little doubt that he knew and profited from these widely-circulated symphonies.

It is a short step from Sammartini to the principal symphonic developments of the mid-eighteenth century. In music as in architecture, north Italy and Austria were strongly connected; many Italians worked in Vienna. With Georg Monn (1717–51) and Georg Christoph Wagenseil (1715–77) the Viennese symphony acquired its own flavour. Monn's symphonies are closer to chamber music, but Wagenseil and Florian Leopold Gassmann (1729–74) were directly affected by their experience in Italian opera. Ignaz Holzbauer (1711–83), a Viennese with a similar background to Wagenseil, moved in 1753 to Mannheim where since 1741 a magnificent orchestra had developed under the direction of the greatest symphonist before Haydn, the Bohemian Johann Stamitz (1717–1757).

Stamitz's education by Jesuits could scarcely have differed more from that afforded by an Italian conservatory; he wrote no operas and very little vocal music of any kind. Instead, as a violin virtuoso, he cultivated instrumental music, including a genre known as the 'violin symphony' – which means no more than that its musical substance was reasonably intelligible from the first violin part. Some of his symphonies are for strings only, but more are for what was becoming a standard orchestral ensemble of two oboes, bassoon, two horns and strings. Flutes or clarinets might be substituted for oboes, and trumpets and drums are occasionally used, but few works before the end of the century employ the fullest ensemble available. Apart from several 'orchestral trio sonatas', there are fifty-eight extant symphonies by Stamitz. In these it is evident that in developing a virtually new genre, he found Italian operas a valuable source of ideas – as later did Mozart and Schubert in their symphonies. Stamitz was

10 'Rittersaal' in the Electoral palace at Mannheim, where Carl Theodor's orchestra performed the symphonies of Stamitz and his colleagues.

immersed in the operatic repertory of Mannheim, in which many of the orchestral devices made famous by his symphonies are already present. Nevertheless his orientation towards domestic 'concert' performance, and his more public concert activity in Paris, tended to loosen the association of the symphony with the theatre. Thus the symphonic mainstream passed from Italy to the German-dominated lands of central Europe. This fact had a profound effect on the nineteenth century; through Haydn and Mozart the symphony became the province of German or German-oriented musicians and Stamitz's achievement paved the way for Beethoven, Spohr, Schubert and their descendants, for all that we call them 'Romantic'.

33

It is only in retrospect that the development of *opera buffa* seems the most powerful generative force in the musical language of the late eighteenth century. At the time, the highest form of musical endeavour remained the heroic drama, nowadays generally termed *opera seria*. The popularity of Metastasio's libretti remained undiminished; new texts were written according to his conventions. Serious Italian opera, like the French *tragédie lyrique* initiated under Louis XIV, mirrors the nobility and magnanimity which the ruling classes believed themselves to possess. Not that the plots lacked conflict. In Metastasio's *La clemenza di Tito*, written for the Emperor's name-day in 1734 (music by the sixty-four-year-old Caldara), Titus is only moved to forgive his would-be assassins after a powerful internal struggle. Villains as well as heroes stem from the ruling classes; they are more often brought to repentance than killed. In Mozart's first *opera seria*, *Mitridate, rè di Ponto*, the king defeats the Romans; before dying of a wound, he is reconciled to his sons, one of them a political enemy, the other his rival in love. Such conflicts can be endlessly permuted without the characters being more than intermittently touched with life. However polished the mechanism of the plot and the verses themselves (Metastasio was a major poet), the Promethean spark eluded most of the composers.

Opera-going was in any case less a dramatic experience than a social occasion or courtly obligation. Some of the great opera houses were among the most important buildings of their cities, although the same operas would often be performed in quite intimate surroundings, for instance in court theatres. The visual spectacle remained a powerful attraction, even when magical effects went out of fashion or became too expensive. The designer was an important member of the team which mounted operas, and was often ahead of the musician and librettist in responding to new artistic currents. For the composer opera was rewarding but irregular work, occasioned by state celebrations or Carnival, which in Catholic countries preceded the closure of the theatres in Lent. For the audience it was magnificent spectacle with unfailingly mellifluous music and the best singing available; the lack of a cutting dramatic edge did not seem fatal.

The deficiencies of *opera seria* are often expressed in terms indebted to Gluck's dedicatory preface to *Alceste* (1769). Nevertheless singers'

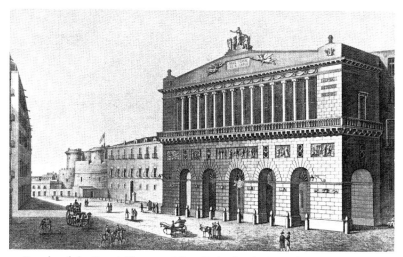

11 Façade of the Royal Theatre of San Carlo (by A. Niccolini, 1810–12, rebuilt 1816), one of the most imposing structures of Naples, in a late and severe Neoclassical idiom.

opera was the proving-ground of the finest composers, such as Metastasio's favourite, Hasse, and Niccolò Jommelli (1714–74), widely considered the greatest Italian composer of his generation. Different composers' settings of the same texts show a remarkable degree of expressive variation. The rigid formal framework, however, was less effective when the musical idiom for which it was designed became obsolete. An advantage for the composer was the confidence that he would be understood so long as he adhered to conventional musical imagery. This may be illustrated by an anecdote about the young Mozart, who was examined at the behest of the Royal Society in 1765:

Suppose, then, a capital speech in Shakespeare never seen before, and yet read by a child of eight years old with all the pathetic energy of a Garrick . . . . I said to the boy, that I should be glad to hear an extemporary *Love Song* . . . . The boy on this . . . looked back with much archness, and immediately began five or six lines of a jargon recitative proper to introduce a love song. He then played a symphony [ritornello] which might correspond with an air composed to the single word, *Affetto*. It had a first and second part, which, together with the symphonies, was of the length that opera songs generally last: if this extemporary composition was not amazingly capital, yet it was really above mediocrity, and shewed most extraordinary readiness of invention.

The feat was repeated with a *Song of Anger* during which 'he had worked himself up to such a pitch, that he beat his harpsichord like a person possessed, rising sometimes in his chair' (Daines Barrington's report on Mozart, received 28 November 1769).

This ability to ape conventional accents goes far to explain how Mozart assimilated so much so quickly; no great master has, on the surface, been so unoriginal as he. But it is symptomatic of the limitations of *opera seria* that the boy reached maturity in this genre so much sooner than in comedy. *Mitridate*, composed for the Carnival at Milan in 1770, is a fine example of the genre, and it pleased the public more than Jommelli's *Armida*, which Mozart heard that year in Naples and declared to be 'beautiful, but too serious and old-fashioned for the theatre'. Jommelli, trained in the old school, combined a mastery of modern vocal and instrumental writing with strict contrapuntal discipline, and his years in Germany had left him out of touch with Italian taste. By 1770 the earliest phase of *style galant* had been superseded by the generation of Niccolò Piccinni (1728–1800) and Antonio Sacchini (1730–86). These composers simplified musical grammar still further, so that while their idiom is evidently founded on that of Vinci's generation, it has become more symmetrical, more clearly cadenced; *galant* ornamentation is fitted to the characteristic modular melodic structure of the mid-century style. Unfailingly smooth, its considerable phrase-span the result of delicate spinning rather than bold development, Piccinni's style was much admired in comic and serious opera, and it made the generation of Jommelli and Gluck seem pompous and contrived, even – the word was used pejoratively at this time – 'baroque'. Today the style seems an effete dilution of a once sturdy idiom, filling out a structure without taking advantage of the most inventive of modern musical styles.

It was unfortunate that changes in the internal form of the aria had no effect on the overall form of *opera seria*. This continued to be the product of a type of libretto devised for the Baroque, even when the arias, which formed the bulk of the music, had taken on *galant* features (indeed Rosen points to the mid-century aria as an influence on the development of instrumental music; see his *Sonata Forms*). Arias remained a potent means of dramatic presentation throughout most of the nineteenth century, but their effect, in the hands of reforming composers and librettists, was enhanced by their appearance as one among many forms. The structure of *opera seria* was, however, occasionally varied at moments of highest pathos, or for the exploration of an individual's dilemma, in orchestrated recitative (*recitativo obbligato*): vocal declamation punctuated by representation of shifting feelings in the orchestra, the music obeying the dictates of the text rather than musical laws of symmetry or development. As Rousseau said:

These passages in which recitative alternates with melody clothed in full orchestral garb are the most moving, the most delectable, the most powerful in all modern music. The actor, stirred, transported by a passion which prevents him saying all he would, pauses, stops, leaves things unsaid, while the orchestra speaks for him; and these silences, thus filled, touch the hearer far more deeply than if the actor himself said everything that the music makes us understand (*Dictionnaire*, 1767).

Both the *recitativo obbligato* and the aria displayed music as an imitative art in accordance with a well-developed Neoclassical theory: music itself is inarticulate, a mere matter of patterns, but combined with words it can plumb the depths of human sentiment.

Enlightenment philosophy paid relatively little attention to instrumental music, but it did fan the flames of reform in serious opera. In France, after demanding (during the 'Querelle des bouffons') the replacement of French serious opera by Italian comedy, the Encyclopaedists proposed that serious drama in French forms should use the modern musical style of Italy: 'We must keep our opera but change our music' (d'Alembert in 1759). In areas already dominated by Italian music, attempts to alter the structure of opera were localized and reflected special conditions. There was no 'operatic reform' covering the spectrum of Italian opera, and in Italy itself the tradition was largely unaffected, proceeding in an unbroken succession from Piccinni through Cimarosa to Rossini.

Jommelli, although a successful composer of *opera buffa*, is most remembered for his original approach to *opera seria*. The special condition in his case was that he worked from 1753 to 1769 at the court of C. P. E. Bach's pupil Duke Carl Eugen at Stuttgart. Jommelli assembled an orchestra rivalling that of nearby Mannheim, and exploited it to the full. It is doubtful whether Jommelli's development can be considered a reform. He used libretti by Metastasio, and others based on mythological subjects, reflecting the influence of contemporary French opera rather than a return to the roots of music drama. He responded fully to the musical stimulus afforded by such subjects, but did not find a new approach to organizing the drama, even in his last work for Stuttgart, *Fetonte* (1768). Jommelli followed Gluck's lead (*Alceste*, 1767) in running the overture into the first act, combining aria with chorus in a single movement, and combining movements into a finale (a procedure perhaps derived from *opera buffa*). But the elaboration of his musical style overwhelms the drama and the work remains in essence a Baroque opera with modern music.

Much the same is true of the best efforts of a younger Neapolitan, Gian Francesco de Majo (1732–70), and of the young Mozart. *Lucio Silla* (Milan, 1772) stretches, but does not break, the traditional mould. In the magnificent tomb scene, an unbroken musical flow and bold harmonic strokes evoke the horror of the place; Cecilio, secretly returned from exile, sings of his hopes and fears; his wife Giunia enters to mourn her father Marius, accompanied by a choral procession. Mozart movingly accommodates himself to the dignified pace of antique ritual – he had seen *Alceste* – and paints details with precision and power (Act I scenes 7–9). The subsequent *galant* duet is a lapse of tone, and the rest of the opera ceases its dangerous flirtation with dramatic intensity and reverts to masterly conventionality.

12 Design by G. C. Bibiena for Gluck's opera *La clemenza di Tito* (1755). Note the lavish detail of set and costumes; but, antedating Neoclassicism, these are thoroughly anachronistic.

The early works of Christoph Willibald von Gluck (1714–87) belong to this class of serious operas which occasionally threaten the framework by sheer musical power. Gluck began his career ordinarily enough. Sent by a patron to Italy in 1737, he studied with Sammartini in Milan and composed operas for north Italian centres. He then visited London, mounting two works in which his proclivity for recycling earlier ideas is already apparent. Lacking fluency, but forced to compete in the market, he used some of his best inventions three times, many finding their final home in his last and greatest operas. The aria 'Se mai senti spirarti' stands out in its original context, *La clemenza di Tito* (Naples, 1752), so irregular in phrasing, and direct in feeling, are its sweeping melody and pulsating accompaniment. In shortened form, it fits superbly into Gluck's last great opera as the aria 'O malheureuse Iphigénie', where the dramatic context is worthy of it (*Iphigénie en Tauride*, 1779). The Metastasian framework simply could not accommodate such musical and dramatic power; it was an archaism by 1760 and although it took another fifty years to die the liveliest developments in serious opera were those which showed dissatisfaction with it. These, however, followed a significant development in comedy.

OPERA BUFFA

By the middle of the century, *opera buffa* had outgrown the self-contained comic interlude and become a full-length entertainment. Metastasio's rigid exclusion of comedy led to its interpolation between the acts. *La serva padrona* consists of two intermezzi designed for a three-act *opera seria*; the heroic world of the latter formed an effective background to the antithesis of middle- and servant-class types, preserving in rational separation what the seventeenth century had freely blended. The launching of comic opera in Italy was achieved by abandoning dialect, after which it found its Metastasio in Carlo Goldoni (1707–93). To Goldoni must go the main credit for the comic opera with serious undertones, the form of Mozart's masterpieces.

Although an extraordinary number of composers emerged from the Naples area, it was in Venice that the new comedy was fully formed. This is not surprising; Venice was a republic, so that an indispensable element of the best comedy, social or political satire, could flourish. Goldoni's libretti bear some relation to earlier types of comedy, including the largely improvised *commedia dell'arte*, but his characters are more fully drawn, as befits an author whose plays continue to hold the stage (Goldoni is a rare instance of an author equally successful in spoken and musical drama). The intrigues, fooling an amorous old man and marrying off a young couple, are archetypal, but Goldoni's works are by no means all farcical. He wrote tragi-comic plays and Metastasian *melodrammi*, and some of his works are close in spirit to the bourgeois comedy later developed in France (Diderot's 'tearful comedy'). Goldoni included serious characters in works designated *dramma giocoso*, as later were *Don Giovanni* and *Così fan tutte*. These graver characters do not join the comic intrigue (or sing in ensembles), but they provide relief from the frivolity and also render tones of comedy which are, in truth, serious, exploring the mind of conventional, sentimental people as well as of the quick-witted and the foolish. A growing confidence in the value of ordinary human characteristics is also exemplified by the genre of the novel, fast-developing at this time. *Opera buffa* was a timely and refreshing alternative to the stylization of *opera seria* and its prototype, Neoclassical French tragedy (which was decaying gradually at this time, its last spark of real life, in the work of Voltaire, preceding its demise by nearly a century).

Goldoni's principal collaborator was Baldassare Galuppi (1706–85), also important as a composer of keyboard and sacred music. Galuppi began with pastoral and serious operas, including some by Metastasio and Goldoni; he visited London shortly before Gluck and maintained a reputation there; later he worked in St Petersburg for three years. He first took advantage of the vogue for Neapolitan comedy, and trained himself by adapting it for the Venetian stage. Galuppi's first important Goldoni comedy was *L'Arcadia in Brenta* (1749). During the 1750s he continued to write *opera seria* for various centres including Rome and Naples, while producing a steady stream of comedies in Venice in which the lines of Classical *opera buffa* were firmly drawn. These include *Il mondo della luna* (1750), *Le virtuose ridicole* (1752), *Il filosofo di campagna* (1754), and *Le pescatrice* (1756).

These works were neither dependent intermezzi nor works for the popular theatre, but a new and sophisticated form. They developed

13 Clowns, by G. D. Tiepolo (the younger), 1727–1804, whose paintings epitomize the Venetian Carnival and the atmosphere of masked intrigue in which *opera buffa* grew to maturity.

new voice-types, notably the tenor and bass ranges, and eschewed the visibly as well as audibly unnatural castrati. Contrasts were developed within a vocal range; sopranos and tenors could now be either comic or sentimental. Comedies were thus differently coloured, but not simpler than *opera seria*. Galuppi's bear no relation to the ballad opera or equivalent popular genres of France, England and Germany; his achievement was to open up for comic purposes musical forms as elaborate as those of serious opera. Galuppi used a variety of aria forms as occasion demanded, but tended to favour a two-strophe design instead of the more massive three-part (da capo) aria of *opera seria*. Comic dialogue occasioned more use of ensemble; whereas in *opera seria* the rare duet is usually an aria for two voices, comedy thrives on duets and larger groups in opposition or misunderstanding.

The main formal innovation was the multi-movement finale. Most of the credit for its invention must go to Goldoni, since much of the design of this most promising of *buffo* forms is inherent in the text. But Galuppi made it popular, and thus an expected convention of *opera buffa*; through his and Piccinni's example it contributed to the later ideal of continuously musical opera. In these finales, a comic situation can develop without the musical sterility of simple recitative; each stage in the imbroglio is fully explored, but quick changes in dramatic fortune can also be accommodated into a musical continuity embracing dialogue, asides, antagonisms, and ensembles of perplexity. It became customary for the succession of movements to accelerate and end with a *prestissimo* during which, however, the action is frozen. Where the words come nearly as fast as in recitative, musical coherence and motion can be assured by independent orchestral development. At worst, the speeding-up of musical-dramatic rhythm will draw an act to a spirited close; at best, these finales exhibit a musical and expressive complexity fully comparable to the finest symphonies. Most people will inevitably think, here, of Mozart, and *Figaro* Act II in particular; but the ingredients of which Mozart made this headiest of his brews had been matured over thirty years.

Galuppi's operas travelled far, but equally significant was the popularity of Goldoni's texts which, like Metastasio's, were set several times. Haydn, for instance, who adapted many operas for the repertory at Esterház, included among his original works *Le pescatrice* (1769); he and Paisiello both set *Il mondo della luna*, respectively in 1777 (Esterház) and 1782 (for Russia). Galuppi was an excellent model, but his dominance did not last. The most popular opera of the 1760s was Piccinni's *La Cecchina, ossia La buona figliuola* (Rome, 1760). Piccinni, a Neapolitan, did not preserve the Venetian's sharp delineation of comic types and differentiation of comedy from *opera seria*, which grew closer together for a time to their mutual disadvantage. *Buffo* elements remain, but the style of the pathetic scenes closely approaches contemporary serious works, such as Piccinni's almost equally celebrated Metastasio opera, *Alessandro nelle Indie* (Rome, 1758). But while *opera seria* became a shadow of its former self, comedy still had considerable life. Goldoni provided the pattern for later librettists such as Bertati (1735–c. 1815). His and Cimarosa's *Il matrimonio segreto* (Vienna, 1792) would be the apogee of eighteenth-century *opera buffa* but for da Ponte and Mozart.

Domenico Cimarosa (1749–1801) and Giovanni Paisiello (1740–1816) prolong this brilliant phase towards the nineteenth century. Although they never touch us deeply, their fertility, melodiousness and sprightliness can still give delight; they are not

14 Final scene from *L'incontro improvviso*, as performed with Haydn's music at Esterház (1775), and directed from the keyboard by the composer; Turkish costumes but a Europeanized rural setting. Note the disposition of the orchestra.

only the most distinguished heirs of Vinci and Pergolesi, but also lead directly to Rossini, who in resetting *Il barbiere di Siviglia* with an adaptation of the libretto set by Paisiello forged the strongest possible connection between Italian *opera buffa* of the eighteenth and early nineteenth centuries. Paisiello's work (St Petersburg, 1782) retains considerable vitality and certainly influenced the setting of its literary sequel by Mozart; it was given in Vienna in 1783. Paisiello composed a *dramma eroicomico*, *Il re Teodoro in Venezia*, for Vienna the following year. His popularity, like that of Martín y Soler (1754–1806) and Antonio Salieri (1750–1825), both of whom collaborated with da Ponte, suggests that his works merit consideration for their own sake, and not just as the background to Mozart's.

The successful composer of Italian opera was probably the most enviable of musicians in the period preceding the French revolutionary wars. At least until Gluck won over both court and public in Paris, the best pickings and the greatest honour were won by those who could attract commissions from the main Italian cities such as Rome and Naples, or the north Italian cities with Austrian connections (Milan, Venice), and then proceed to fortune in Vienna, London, Berlin or Russia without necessarily renouncing appointments at home. The new Russian capital, St Petersburg, gave extended welcomes to Galuppi, Traetta, Sarti, Cimarosa and Paisiello. Such appointments were not without danger after 1790; Cimarosa, Piccinni, and Paisiello all fell foul of authority and died in less than comfortable circumstances. But each had shone cometlike over musical Europe, with a trail of glory scarcely equalled before by any composer.

CHAPTER THREE

Other operatic traditions; operatic reform

The principal forms of Italian opera were the serious and comic types capable of being mounted anywhere. There also survived a specialized form descended directly from the great feasts of the Renaissance, a form closer to the continuing tradition in France, and which hardly travelled at all. Making use of expensive stage machinery and of chorus and dance, as well as the vocal virtuosity common to all forms of Italian opera, wealthy courts mounted a *festa teatrale* or *azione teatrale* on special occasions, based on mythological subjects capable of being understood allegorically. Ostensibly old-fashioned, they were more in tune than *opera seria* with the Neoclassical aesthetic, and within this framework, and using the favourite subject of the earliest operas, the Orpheus legend, there came into focus a movement often called the 'reform' of Italian opera.

The case should not be oversimplified. Gluck's *Orfeo ed Euridice* (1762) is not a typical *festa*. Normally the *festa* is replete with full-length arias no less ornate than those of *opera seria*. There was no opposition between the genres; in Vienna, Metastasio, as Caesarian poet, wrote texts for both. His *Alcide al bivio*, set by Hasse, was performed in 1760 for the wedding of the future Joseph II. Gluck himself contributed *Le cinesi* (1754), an *azione* by Metastasio, for performance by the royal family: in it three Chinese maidens indulge the conceit of playing out dramatic scenes in observance of Western conventions. Soon, however, Gluck was directed down another path. For the Emperor's birthday in 1755 he composed *L'innocenza giustificata*, a one-act *festa* with recitative texts by the theatre manager Count Durazzo. The arias were taken from various works of Metastasio, suggesting a lack of confidence (which displeased the poet) in the organic relation of his arias to their original dramatic context. The result is not entirely satisfactory. Stirrings of reform cannot be detected in the recitatives and long arias which form most of the work, but only at the dramatic climax. The heroine, condemned to die for neglecting the sacred flame, sings a simple, touching prayer; the musical form is left unfinished when the goddess miraculously rekindles the fire. In 1756 Gluck wrote his last Metastasian *opera seria* (*Antigono*, for Rome) and set *Il re pastore* for the Emperor's birthday. By now well established at court, Gluck was responsible for performances of many works over the next few years, including some by Traetta; meanwhile he devoted much of his energy to French comic operas.

The most serious efforts at reforming Italian opera during the 1750s were those of the *philosophe* Francesco Algarotti (1712–64) and the composer Tommaso Traetta (1727–79). Algarotti published his *Saggio sopra l'opera in musica* in 1755; it was translated, reprinted and widely read. He not only attacked the prevailing sloppiness of Italian theatres, but proposed a reform amounting to nothing less than a Neoclassical vision; and he took the practical step of providing a model libretto, perversely but prophetically in French. Algarotti's proposal coincided with the beginnings of Neoclassicism, stimulated by the growing popularity of archaeology. The *Saggio* appeared in the same year as the first Rome journey of Johann Joachim Winckelmann (1717–68), who definitively formulated a concept of antique beauty characterized by nobility and serenity (ill. 1), the antithesis, in German thought of the late eighteenth century, of the turbulence of *Sturm und Drang*. Algarotti extended his ideas to architecture; opera houses, he argued, should be purged of decorative excess and be built simply in Neoclassical forms. His libretto was inspired by Neoclassical French tragedy; it was, indeed, an *Iphigenia in Aulis*, in which elevated feelings, the spirit of patriotism and self-sacrifice, inform characters who vary between the innocent and the heroic (Iphigenia and Achilles), the subtle (Calchas, the priest), and the mature and complex (Clytemnestra, Agamemnon). Instead of the *opera seria* formula, a tangled situation unravelled by improbable changes of heart, the characters accept their destiny, their inevitable collision averted by divine intervention. Intrigue is banished or reduced to Agamemnon's ruses which have the noble aim of saving his daughter. The background to the plot is that unless Diana is propitiated by the sacrifice of Iphigenia, the Greek force cannot sail for Troy. Like many other critics, Algarotti was impressed by French staging and flexibility of musical forms, and accordingly employed the choral and dance elements neglected in *opera seria*.

15 'The Artist Moved by the Grandeur of Ancient Ruins' by Henry Fuseli (1778–9). Classical antiquity is handled with virtually a Romantic awe in the decade of *Sturm und Drang*.

Although it seems never to have been used, Algarotti's libretto inspired others including that of Gluck's first Paris opera. But the first fruits of his ideas were translations into Italian of French librettos, in which Algarotti played a part. These were initially staged at the Bourbon court of Parma, where the manager, du Tillot, was French. The court composer was Traetta, who had trained in Naples and been in contact with Jommelli, contributing arias to a Naples production of his *Ifigenia in Aulide* (a pre-Algarotti version by Matteo Verazi, who favoured mythological subjects even when working within an *opera seria* framework as in Jommelli's *Fetonte*).

In Parma (from 1758), Traetta worked with the local poet Frugoni on *Ippolito ed Aricia* and *I tintaridi* (1759 and 1760), translated from the libretti of Rameau's first two operas. Traetta used some of Rameau's dances, but composed the vocal sections, reshaping several scenes to conform to Italian expectations. In 1761 Traetta's *Armida*, translated by Durazzo and Migliavacca from Quinault's libretto (set by Lully, 1686), was given at the Vienna Burgtheater. Traetta followed these translations with libretti by Verazi (*Sofonisba*; Mannheim, 1762) and Marco Coltellini (*Ifigenia in Tauride*; Vienna, 1763) designed to allow scope for 'French' elements, ballet and chorus. *Ifigenia* was Traetta's most widely-known serious opera; it was followed up by Coltellini with another superb Neoclassical tragedy, *Antigone*, set by Traetta for St Petersburg in 1772.

47

Traetta's achievement at its best constitutes a musical and dramatic synthesis of French forms with the *lingua franca* of Italian opera. He continued to set conventional libretti, serious and comic; but his uniqueness in his 'reform' works was recognized in the antique colouring, and a breadth of design, both of which affected Gluck. Some of Traetta's great scenes, like Sofonisba's suicide or the funeral rite in *Antigone*, are as moving as the tomb scene in *Lucio Silla*, and match the greatest Gluck. Unfortunately, if we apply Gluck's standards, Traetta's successes are intermittent; he had too ready a recourse to the *opera seria* style, even the da capo aria.

Traetta was willingly led into reform by circumstances and particular librettists. The same is true of Gluck who, however, had the luck to work over several years in cosmopolitan Vienna. His period of experimentation was longer, his experience more varied, and if he was less gifted musically than Traetta he learned to conserve his energies to maximum effect, allowing nothing to impede dramatic momentum. At first directed by Durazzo, the choreographer Gasparo Angiolini (1731–1803), and his principal librettist Raniero da Calzabigi (1714–95), Gluck learned from them all until, in his French works, he himself became the dramatist. It is with the establishment of the composer, rather than the poet or singer, as the architect and controlling force, that modern opera came of age; and this was largely Gluck's achievement.

Gluck's first completely reformist work was the ballet *Don Juan* (1761). Angiolini proclaimed his intentions in the first of the manifestos associated with Gluck's progress; quite possibly this, like later ones signed by Gluck himself, was drafted by Calzabigi. Ballet was to become an expressive medium, instead of decorative entertainment, through the use of pantomime: gesture and facial expression as well as bodily movement allowed it to handle any subject-matter. The choreography of *Don Juan* cannot be recovered, but its nature can be inferred from the libretto and the acting style developed for Shakespearian tragedy by Garrick. The dramatic *ballet d'action* was claimed as his invention by J. G. Noverre, while Angiolini asserted the priority of his mentor Franz Hilverding. Angiolini staged several ballets with music by Gluck, including *Iphigenia in Aulis*; the music, apparently lost, may even be in the opera of that name since much of the ballet *Semiramis* (1765) reappears in *Iphigénie en Tauride*.

In 1762 the Emperor's name-day was celebrated with the *azione teatrale Orfeo ed Euridice*, in which the guiding hand was Calzabigi's. A period in Paris, during which he published an edition of Metastasio, had enabled Calzabigi to assimilate the French tradition; now, with Durazzo's support, he could develop his own considerable poetic gifts in continuation of an anti-Metastasian movement. In *Orfeo* he collaborated with the Quaglios, the most innovative and resourceful theatrical designers of the time, Angiolini, the castrato Guadagni, an acting-pupil of Garrick, and of course Gluck. Gluck never denied Calzabigi the credit for drawing together the threads of reform. Nevertheless, while *Orfeo* was the fruit of many talents and one of the most remarkable theatrical events of the century, as a total art-work it is beyond recall; and it owes its survival to Gluck's music.

It is a common misunderstanding to regard *Orfeo* as a contribution to the reform of the *opera seria*. In fact it stands outside it altogether, a masterpiece of the pastoral tradition. It is Gluck's response to Calzabigi's ideas about declamation that marks it off from other festive operas. 'The chevalier Gluck is simplifying music': ten years

16 C. W. von Gluck, part of 'Che farò senz'Euridice', the culminating aria in *Orfeo*; the original version, from the first edition (Paris, 1764).

later Burney tells us how Gluck appeared in an age dominated by Hasse and Jommelli. He reported Gluck as saying that he had modelled himself on the good taste of the English, but this may have been flattery: Handel had no noticeable effect on him for twenty years. It was Calzabigi's admiration for French opera combined with Gluck's experience in *opéra comique* which led to a style purged of superfluous ornament in which the melodic line is closely modelled on the text and gives it full poetic value. Gluck was later to remark: 'I have striven to be more poet and painter than musician'. In effect he usurped the functions of painter and poet, endowing the verse with directness and truth of expressive accent, and unforgettably limning, in a few strokes, the atmosphere of each scene.

Gluck's subsequent works have led to accusations of backsliding. He had no reason, however, to regard *Orfeo* as a manifesto, and he continued for a few years to fulfil relatively conventional commissions. Although he wrote no more *opere serie*, never wrote an *opera buffa*, and after 1764 composed no more *opéras comiques*, he produced two festive works with texts by Metastasio, and in 1769 with Frugoni at Parma, *Le feste d'Apollo* into which a shortened version of *Orfeo* was incorporated. *Telemacco*, written with Coltellini for Vienna in 1765, mingles reformed structures with magical scenes in French taste. The real turning-point was the publication in 1769 of the true manifesto of reform, the prefatory dedication to the Duke of Tuscany of the tragedy *Alceste*. Significantly, although the traditional libretto is also a target, the primary object of scorn is the musical excess of *opera seria*: its abandonment of poetic values to appease the vanity of singers and its expansion of musical forms at the expense of dramatic sense and continuity.

Alceste, performed in Vienna in 1767, follows Traetta's path; it is an alternative form of *opera seria*. But Calzabigi and Gluck went much further in their complete abandonment of *galant* style in favour of the more austere Neoclassicism. Their source was Euripides' drama, but they turned it into a majestic Aeschylean dramatic machine; the extended tableaux of *Orfeo* (which do not exceed equivalent scenes in Traetta) are developed into huge static blocks of material bound together by repetitions of fully-developed choruses. Leopold Mozart, who saw it with his son early in 1768, referred to 'the sad opera *Alceste*', and it is indeed the most unremittingly sombre of all operas. A slight relief is provided by the divertissement at the King's recovery

M. Gluck has developed his ideas of the neceſſary requiſites of dramatic muſic ſo fully, in his dedication of *Alceſte*, to the Grand Duke of Tuſcany; and has given his reaſons for deviating from the beaten track, with ſo much force and freedom, that I ſhall make no apology for preſenting my readers, with an extract from it.

"When I undertook to ſet this poem, "it was my deſign to diveſt the muſic "entirely of all thoſe abuſes with which "the vanity of ſingers, or the too great "complacency of compoſers, has ſo long "disfigured the Italian opera, and ren- "dered the moſt beautiful and magnifi- "cent of all public exhibitions, the moſt "tireſome and ridiculous. It was my "intention to confine muſic to its true "dramatic province, of aſſiſting poe- "tical

17 Gluck, dedication to *Alceste*, translated in Burney's *The Present State of Music in Germany*. It continues: '. . . poetical expression, and of augmenting the interest of the fable, without interrupting the action, or chilling it with useless and superfluous ornament'.

from illness, but this is ironic: the price of his cure is the death of his wife. Alkestis visits the underworld to plead for a short reunion with her husband; she addresses the spirits of death in an aria ('Ombre, larve') whose musical material is so simple that contrasts of scale in the orchestra, of vocal range, and chordal blocks, become the principal themes. Elsewhere Gluck's melody is made powerful by restraint, while his instrumentation goes beyond *Orfeo* in dramatic use of sonority (notably the chalumeau and trombones). With its choral mass, its ballet, its happy ending brought about by divine intervention, *Alceste* is a natural sequel to *Orfeo*; nevertheless it represents a breakdown in collaborative harmony. Apart from the ritual in Act I the dances are far less well integrated and the choreographer, Noverre, went his own way and provided a 'grotesque ballet'.

Above all, in *Alceste*, the musician found a positive role. While Gluck failed to overcome Calzabigi's longueurs by recitative, his choral and aria complexes completely dominate the verse. *Alceste*, in its original form, is at once Gluck's greatest achievement and his most intolerable. In 1776 he rewrote it for Paris virtually from scratch, and in the process rendered it more human, theatrically more viable, less intransigently monumental. The revision entailed losses as well as gains, however, and the original form stands as the purest achievement of Neoclassicism in music drama.

The laws and patents restraining music theatre in France contributed to the resistance to change which characterized French opera through most of the eighteenth century. Lully's operas remained the model for the *tragédie lyrique*, and many were revived, *Thésée* as late as 1779. Well into the nineteenth century, the institution for which Lully composed, the 'Académie Royale de Musique' or 'Opéra', jealously guarded its exclusive right to produce dramatic works with continuous music. Repeated bans were placed on troupes attempting too elaborate a form of music theatre. The 'fair theatres' (*théâtres de la foire*) flourished in the environs of Paris, playing simple dramas interspersed with popular tunes, and there were several attempts at establishing a permanent Opéra-Comique company. The movement gathered pace, however, only after the 'Querelle des bouffons'. The appearance of *La serva padrona*, played by a visiting Italian *buffo* troupe between the acts of a Lully opera, provided the perfect occasion for a war of words: the contrast between heavy French tragedy (its performance slowed down by the accretion of modern ornamentation) and slick Italian comedy was irresistible. This 'Querelle' was pointless – it did not compare like with like – but its consequences were far-reaching. While *tragédie lyrique* and the festive *opéra-ballet* continued almost unchallenged, Pergolesi's sparkling little opera pointed the way for an indigenous form of comedy. Rousseau, who was to declare in his *Letter on French Music* (1753) that French was an impossible language for singing, had already set his own text to unpretentious music in *Le devin du village*, a unique composition owing very little to Italian models except that it included recitatives. Its successor was *Les troqueurs* (1753) by Antoine Dauvergne (1713–97), who pretended his more elaborate music was an Italian opera translated. Yet Dauvergne continued to compose Lullian operas, initiating in 1758 the practice of newly setting old libretti for the Opéra (*Enée et Lavinie*).

Les troqueurs showed Dauvergne's knowledge of a modern instrumental as well as vocal style. Outside the Opéra, Paris was already the home of an advanced symphonic tradition; Stamitz was there in 1754–5 and François-Joseph Gossec (1734–1829) began writing symphonies in 1756 for the private orchestra of the financier La Pouplinière. Whereas in Italy and Germany the development of symphony and opera were linked, in France the life of the many concert-giving organizations was independent, and stylistic developments went their own way although important personalities were involved in both fields.

It is typical of French operatic history that the composers who established the artistically mature *opéra comique* were an Italian working in Paris, Egidio Duni (1708–75), and an Austrian, Gluck, working in Vienna. The reasons for this simultaneous development lay partly in the appearance of a good librettist, Charles Simon Favart (1710–92), after whom the Opéra-Comique in Paris is still named 'Salle Favart'. Favart began with musical theatre of the lighter kind, although his *Don Quichotte* (1743), with music by Boismortier, was written for the Opéra. He worked for the *opéra-comique* companies and the fair theatres, which he developed from improvised theatre with songs into *comédie mêlée d'ariettes*, a designation still applied much later to what is now generally termed *opéra comique*. 'Comique' does not mean 'humorous'. Nevertheless at least until the Revolution *opéra comique* is mostly antithetical to the style of the Opéra, at which it sometimes poked fun. In the aftermath of the 'Querelle', Favart translated Italian works and wrote new French texts, which were composed, usually for the singularly ill-named 'Comédie Italienne', by Duni, Philidor, Monsigny and Grétry. His work was also exported. From 1752 there existed a 'French theatre near the Court' in Vienna, and under Durazzo's management its musical activities increased to include adaptations of plays with *ariettes*. Not all the libretti were Favart's, but he was Durazzo's agent in supplying them. Gluck cemented his relationship with the court by adapting music for these texts from 1756; later he composed fresh music.

In 1756 Duni, who may have known Favart's work at Parma, requested a libretto from the director of the reconstituted Opéra-Comique, Jean Monnet, and received Anseaume's *Le peintre amoureux de son modèle*. Duni came to Paris for the performance and stayed, setting a text by Favart, *La fille mal gardée*, and composing or collaborating in three other operas before the end of 1758. In this year Gluck composed *La fausse magie* (partly by Anseaume) and Anseaume's *L'île de Merlin*, first in a series of eight French comedies ending with *La rencontre imprévue* in 1764. *La rencontre* is an example of a popular subject, an adventure taking place within the confines of Europe's exotic neighbour, the Turkish Empire. It is also the first full-length masterpiece of *opéra comique*.

Duni, a contemporary of Pergolesi, contributed to the increasing Italianization of the music of *opéra comique*; he was not, however, a subtle composer and it is not surprising that his leading role in the new operatic form was quickly ceded to a young Frenchman. François-André Danican Philidor (1726–95) returned to Paris in the mid-1750s after a period abroad in which he became known as the finest chess-player of the age, and also assimilated the newest Italian musical style. Working mainly with Sedaine (1719–97), the best of Favart's successors, he produced a series of ingeniously wrought comedies beginning with *Blaise le savetier* in 1759. Most of them are in one act, but *Le maréchal ferrant* (1764) and *Le sorcier* are in two and with *Tom Jones* (1765), another adaptation of an English novel, Philidor expanded into three acts. Philidor's development of *opéra comique* is a musical one; in common with most of his peers, he showed little sign of taking command dramatically, and the aesthetic result, despite his musical brilliance, is often spoiled through the ineptitude of another librettist, Poinsinet. Philidor made skilful use of a simple orchestra (notably the wind instruments then often neglected), and on the basis of a thoroughly Italian motivic contrapuntal technique showed how multiple musical characters can be combined in an ensemble. His versatility in this respect was unrivalled: a duet in different metres, quintets, septets, effortlessly develop the volubly expressed opinions of characters at loggerheads. The finale to Act II of *Tom Jones* is a *tour de force*. Philidor also introduced elements from *opera seria*. In Act III of *Tom Jones* Sophia sings an obbligato recitative and full-length aria in the best possible position, where a personal crisis brings on the deepest introspection. Significantly, however, it is shorn of vocal virtuosity; the performers were still singing actors, the French equivalents of the *opera buffa* players who performed Gluck's *Alceste*.

Philidor's supremacy did not long remain unchallenged. The first *opéra comique* of Pierre-Alexandre Monsigny (1729–1817) also dates from 1759, and like Philidor's first was a success at a fair theatre.

Whereas Philidor sprang from one of France's great musical dynasties, Monsigny was a musical amateur; but he possessed theatrical sense, and a melodic spontaneity which compensated for a lack of sophistication. His vein of pathos was unmatched in *opéra comique* before Grétry. Hence Monsigny played a major part in turning *opéra comique*, barely past its first decade, towards more serious subjects. In 1768 Duni had set Favart's version of the biblical story of Ruth (*Les moissonneurs*). The tearful *opéra comique*, matching the spoken *comédie larmoyante*, then moved to its natural bourgeois level in Monsigny's *Le déserteur* (by Sedaine, 1769), his greatest triumph, exploiting the tension of placing a leading character under sentence of death and delaying his reprieve until the last moment.

Opéra comique remained the liveliest form in Paris until Gluck in 1774 breathed new life into the Opéra. With the next generation, established by Grétry's first work in 1768, the comic genre remained, like *opera buffa*, subject to modification rather than fundamental change. André Ernest Modeste Grétry (1741–1813) was trained in Italy – he claimed to have walked there from his native Liège – but he began his successful career in Paris in collaboration with Marmontel and Sedaine. His musical style made a virtue of simplicity; he was a declared disciple of Rousseau and *Le devin du village*, and theorized about the relation of words and music in a manner with which Philidor, a more gifted musician, would never have concerned himself. Grétry took part in a diversification of subject matter in *opéra comique* which prepared for its more serious role under the Revolution. A highly successful oriental fantasy (Marmontel's *Zémire et Azor*, 1771) satisfied the taste for the 'marvellous' in an epoch of second-rate 'serious' opera. This tale of 'Beauty and the Beast' mingles the 'tearful' (Zémire), buffoonery (the servant Ali), heroism (Azor), and solid bourgeois virtue (Zémire's father). It also includes scenic effects and dancing as integral elements. It was natural that Grétry should soon turn his attention to the Opéra, in *Céphale et Procris* (Marmontel, 1773), a pastoral, rather than tragic, watering-down of the cruel tale from Ovid. Grétry's main triumph on the Opéra stage was an oriental comedy, *Le caravane du Caire*, which attained over five hundred performances; when he essayed the high style of Gluck (*Andromaque*, 1780) he was not true to his own genius, which was for pastel shades. Grétry learned from Philidor's ingenuity, combining two choruses in *Colinette à la cour* (1782), and use of Italianate aria, as in his most popular work, *Richard Coeur-de-lion* (Sedaine, 1784). This work capitalizes on the taste for chivalric romance; the imprisoned Richard communes with himself in a simplified version of the Italian idiom, Grétry's conscious response to the doctrines of the Encyclopaedists. By 1784, however, this style was well established at the Opéra itself.

Opéra comique flourished in France because it filled a vacuum in the theatrical life of a nation uniquely resistant to Italian opera. It benefitted also from the growing middle-class audience who at first enjoyed seeing themselves on the stage, and later accepted heroism and magic as a natural part of operatic experience so long as the situations were clear and strong, and the characters remained human rather than mythological. A sufficient literary tradition, with Favart, Sedaine, and Marmontel, supported the composers (it is a pity the most entertaining dramatist of the time, Beaumarchais, did not write *opéra comique*), as did critics such as Diderot. French musical comedy became an exportable commodity; French was the most widely understood language of European cities and in any case works with spoken dialogue are comparatively simple to translate into the vernacular.

Such a fortunate constellation of conditions did not occur elsewhere, and opera in the vernacular, while much cultivated in the last half of the eighteenth century, failed even in Germany to oust the Italians. There were, nevertheless, distinct traditions related to *opéra comique* in England, Spain and Russia. The continuing popularity of *The Beggar's Opera* (1728) maintained the possibility of English musical comedy in parallel to the mainly serious Italian opera. Like *The Beggar's Opera*, Arne's *Love in a Village* (1762) included popular and operatic songs parodied for a text refurbished by Isaac Bickerstaffe. Arne's successors, such as Charles Dibdin (1745–1814) and the young Thomas Linley (1756–78), Mozart's boyhood friend who tragically drowned, elaborated the musical idiom. Linley's *The Duenna* (Covent Garden, 1775) retained many traditional melodies to which Sheridan fitted his words, but accompanied them in *galant* style. Dibdin's lively tunefulness enabled him to reject the support of inherited tunes. During the 1770s the London musical theatre promised as much as the French ten years before, despite the loss in 1772 of Bickerstaffe, forced like so many of his profession to escape creditors in exile. But with William Shield (1748–1829), who followed Arne in adapting an Italianate style to English words, and Stephen Storace (1762–96), who was half-Italian, an associate of Mozart, and had written an opera to a text by da Ponte (*Gli equivoci*, Vienna, 1786), the *galant* style and native simplicity failed to blend into a rejuvenated national idiom as they had in France. Had these composers enjoyed the support of the wealthiest and most articulate patrons of opera, continuing operatic activity in English might have produced something worthy to rank with the century-old work of Purcell. Snobbery, the preference of a trading nation for imported wares, remained a discouraging factor in British musical life for another century.

In Spain and Russia the higher echelons of society were equally prone to import opera from Italy rather than encourage local products. Nevertheless this low period in Spain's political influence began with considerable activity in the local form of *opéra comique*, the *zarzuela*. In contrast, however, to France, the Italian tide rose high in Spain and in the most talented Spanish opera composer, Martín y Soler, who worked in Vienna, London and Russia. The *zarzuela* died, therefore, at the very time that new life entered other vernacular traditions. It is perhaps a reflection of the greater vitality of Russian civilization that her entry into European affairs, which coincided with the adoption of Western architecture, manners and (by the ruling classes) language, was nevertheless accompanied by growth in Russian-language opera. Despite the importation of Italian and French music and musicians, the folk melodies of Russia and the Ukraine were adapted for operatic use. The long arm of the Enlightenment penetrated even here; *Le devin du village* having been given in Moscow in 1778, a Russian descendant, *The Miller-Magician*, appeared the following year. Even its overture is based on folk melodies, their rude vigour tamed towards symmetrical periodicity in *galant* taste. The comedies generally employed the pastoral and bourgeois settings enjoyed in the West, but a wider range of subject-matter appears in the chief Russian composer of the time, Evstigney Ipatovich Fomin (1761–1800). Not only did Fomin, like Dibdin, compose in a folk-like or *galant* idiom as required, he went outside the comic style altogether in *Orpheus and Eurydice* (1792). Despite his early death the repertory continued to expand, and the work of the Venetian Cavos and the Russian Davidov must be counted, well before the selfconsciously Romantic nationalism of Glinka, among the foundations of one of opera's great traditions.

Germany was not a nation but a linguistic unit which embraced a multiplicity of political systems and even, unlike Italy, a religious schism. In retrospect, German musical culture of the eighteenth century appears second to none in variety and depth. But political considerations, not least the wars occasioned by the aggrandizement of Prussia under Frederick II, militated against the consistent cultivation of a genre which allows the composer to cut his teeth on imitation and to fail without losing hope of future success. Germany possessed a strong tradition of improvised entertainment of the *commedia dell'arte* type. In the buffooneries of Hanswurst, the comic plays of Faust and Don Juan, an indigenous tradition of light theatre and travelling companies existed upon which opera might have capitalized more effectively. Haydn worked with such troupes at Esterház; Schikaneder ran one, before settling in Vienna; Weber learned his trade as a member of one. But the very mobility of such troupes was an obstacle to consistent artistic development, or even to presenting major new works; *The Magic Flute* would never have been written on the road.

Otherwise there was little native opera in mid-century Germany. The influential courts, like Berlin and Vienna, were Italian-dominated; if the chief composers such as Graun in Berlin and Hasse in Dresden were German, they, like Handel and J. C. Bach in London, were musically colonists from Italy. The lesser courts followed suit, unless they inclined towards France or blended the cultures, like Stuttgart. *Singspiel* – which meant simply 'opera in German' but has come to mean German opera with spoken dialogue and is used in that sense here – languished or was artificially cultivated in a few centres. Mannheim, for instance, possessed links with Paris, but its court presented mainly Italian opera including imported works and new commissions (J. C. Bach, *Temistocle* and *Lucio Silla*, 1772 and 1774). In the town French opera was popular during the season when the court retired to Schwetzingen. But Mannheim also offered hospitality to German opera. The *Alkeste* of Anton Schweitzer (1735–87), first given at Weimar in 1773, came to Mannheim in 1775, and two years later the resident Kapellmeister Holzbauer produced *Günther von Schwarzburg*. These, however, were essentially German-texted *opere serie*, a genre in which Holzbauer already had experience; such, indeed, was the conscious aim of the librettist of *Alkeste*, Wieland. The use of the German language occasioned some simplification of style but the approach resembled more the musically elaborated *opere serie* of Jommelli than the reformed style of Gluck, whose last operatic work, however, was the German translation of *Iphigénie en Tauride* (Vienna, 1781).

Stylistically, German opera received a more vital stimulus from opera with spoken dialogue, which also benefitted as much from outside influence as from its own shallow roots. It was not until the next century, when the continual threat of invasion and control by France fostered German national consciousness, that the plant was fully established in German soil. While opera in German grew in popularity during the last quarter of the eighteenth century, much of it was in translation. Gluck's *La rencontre imprévue* was widely performed in a German translation first heard at Frankfurt in 1772. Later, Mozart's *Don Giovanni* was performed far more often, in the composer's lifetime and up to 1800, as *Don Juan, ein Singspiel*, with spoken dialogue completely different from da Ponte's recitative.

Mozart himself showed continual interest in German opera, although he rarely had the opportunity to compose one. As a boy of twelve he set Favart's version of the tale told by Rousseau in *Le devin*; *Bastien und Bastienne* was privately performed in Vienna in 1768. In 1777 he witnessed and admired *Günther von Schwarzburg*. He also liked a new form, melodrama, possibly devised by Rousseau, whose *Pygmalion* was translated into German and given at Weimar in 1772 with Schweitzer's music. Melodrama was cultivated by Georg Benda (1722–95) in *Ariadne* and *Medea* (both 1775) and *Pygmalion* (1779). The text is spoken, but divided by orchestral material in the manner of *recitativo obbligato*; the composer was thus spared the problem of adapting recitative style, devised for the Italian language, to German prosody. Mozart was very excited by the idea, which, he said, ought to be used for all German recitatives. In *Zaïde* (1779–80) he employed it at a dramatic crux, but this *Singspiel*, which includes some wonderful music, was never finished. Although melodrama was used in Mozart's music for *Thamos, King of Egypt* (1776–9) and later in Beethoven's incidental music (notably *Egmont*, 1810) and in one scene of *Fidelio*, it was not used consistently in Mozart's mature German operas and never attained the position he predicted.

By the end of the century German composers were acceptable

abroad without having to disguise themselves in Italian or French dress. J. M. Kraus (1756–92) in Sweden, and J. A. P. Schulz (1747–1800), who composed operas on the contemporary land reform in Denmark, may be only footnotes in operatic history, but they symbolized the maturation of German music even as they helped sow the seeds of Scandinavian national identities. Germans like J. C. Vogel and Peter Winter followed Gluck in composing serious French operas. But the first masterpiece of Classical German opera remains Mozart's *Die Entführung aus dem Serail* (Vienna, 1782), a work so eclectic in conception that it did little to establish a national idiom.

Yet *Die Entführung* was commissioned following a 1776 decree of Joseph II intended to stimulate the production of German operas in a 'National Theatre'. The experiment was discontinued soon after Mozart's opera appeared. Nevertheless *Die Entführung* was his most widely-performed opera in his lifetime, and marked a high point in his fortunes in Vienna; if the Emperor himself said it had 'too many notes', it was admired by the generally parsimonious Gluck. It represents a stage beyond *La rencontre imprévue* or the works of Grétry in the sophistication of its musical means to the point of being over-written. When a singer waits for sixty bars of ritornello, in effect a sinfonia concertante for flute, oboe, violin and cello, before beginning her aria ('Marten aller Arten'), one may well ask if the Emperor was not right. Mozart showed himself a master of the exotic setting, with the 'Turkish' music of the overture and choruses, the irascible Osmin, guardian of the harem, and Pedrillo's serenade which signals the attempted escape. But the leading figures, Konstanze and Belmonte, seem to have stepped out of a more opulent genre, and the Pasha, on whose supposed severity and actual clemency the plot turns, is a speaking role. It would be idle to seek here for clues to that mysterious sense of organic unity possible in opera sung throughout; only in *The Magic Flute* did Mozart apparently relish, and actually take advantage of, the inorganic nature of *Singspiel*. Nevertheless *Die Entführung* is a fascinating opera, and with the vastly comic Osmin, the pert maid Blonde, and the brilliant quartet finale to Act II, it is an essential step towards Mozart's great masterpieces of *opera buffa*.

CHAPTER FOUR

Classical opera at its height

After *Alceste* Gluck pursued a winding road without looking back. In *Alceste* he had restored a limited amount of simple recitative, whereas there was none in *Orfeo*. He again banished it in his last opera by Calzabigi, *Paride ed Elena* (Vienna, 1770); but the castrato, omitted from *Alceste*, returns for the role of Paris, the lover whose direct, song-like style makes appropriate the singing voice *par excellence*. *Paride* remains the Cinderella among Gluck's mature works. He was especially proud of having distinguished musically the Trojans and the Spartans, providing a model for the cultivation of national characteristics in many later operas, but he made no attempt to present this work in France.

Gluck had determined that the right place to launch his reform before a wider public was Paris, but the Opéra was reluctant to entertain him; luckily Marie-Antoinette, Dauphine of France, was his pupil, and her intervention overcame the objections of the opera director, Dauvergne. He, however, stipulated that Gluck should write six French operas, to replace the hallowed repertory which would not survive the comparison. Gluck accordingly produced *Iphigénie en Aulide* and a French version of *Orfeo* in 1774; the French *Alceste* in 1776; and in 1777, *Armide*, a setting of Quinault's libretto of 1686. He also adapted two of his Viennese *opéras comiques*. Nevertheless two more operas were insisted upon, and in 1779 he produced *Iphigénie en Tauride* and *Echo et Narcisse*.

Gluck's French campaign was carefully planned, but it encountered opposition, first from traditionalists, then from the ultra-Italian party. The latter feared Gluck more than old French opera, for he was Italian-trained and represented the international (Italian) style; yet he was not himself Italian and his priorities were dramatic, not sensuously musical. Gluck won sweeping successes, especially with *Orphée* and *Tauride*, while only the pastoral *Echo* was a failure. He overwhelmed an embryonic French reform movement, led by Philidor (*Ernelinde*, 1767) and Gossec (*Sabinus*, 1773), composers who might have made headway in the aftermath of Gluck had not Paris been swept by a wave of Italians. Two works of Sacchini were translated by Framery and staged with spoken dialogue. Then Piccinni was thrust unwillingly into the fray; arriving in Paris at the end of 1776, he was taught French by Marmontel and set to work on *Roland*, adapted from Quinault's libretto of 1685. Marmontel also prepared the way by denouncing Gluck as a mere German whose crude and over-intellectual music was disliked in Italy; France, in her belated conversion to true Italian melody, must learn to recognize the real thing. Scurrilous as it is, Marmontel's *Essai* was the work of a considerable literary stylist, and it appeared when the French were by no means sure how much they liked *Alceste*. Marmontel was supported by la Harpe, a pedantic Neoclassical dramatist and theorist, who believed that music could not, or should not, attempt to be seriously dramatic; he particularly detested *Armide*, describing the heroine's role as a monotonous and fatiguing shriek. *Roland*, too, was a success in 1778.

Gluck expressed indignation at French ingratitude, but he probably enjoyed the fray, and he had plenty of able supporters. He refused to set *Roland* in competition with Piccinni; and when the latter was offered *Iphigénie en Tauride* as his second French opera with the assurance that it would appear before Gluck's, the management broke its word rather than affront the 'German Orpheus'. Piccinni's *Iphigénie* appeared only in 1781, and Gluck's was promptly revived to its detriment. Yet Gluck had cleared the way for Italian music, and Piccinni now resided in Paris, producing several new operas of which the most successful were *Atys* (1780) and *Didon* (1783) (ill. 37). He also taught singing, presented Italian operas, and wrote *opéras comiques*. Sacchini came in person, and his *Oedipe à Colone*, presented posthumously in 1787, was the most successful opera of the decade, remaining in the repertory for over five hundred performances. Salieri's *Les Danaïdes* was billed as partly by Gluck (1784); it led to two further operas, one with a text intended for Gluck by Beaumarchais (*Tarare*, 1787, adapted by da Ponte for Vienna as *Axur*).

None of the Italians, however, displaced Gluck as the master of this remarkable revival in the fortunes of the Paris Opéra, for it was he who converted it from a museum into a place of musical novelty and dramatic vitality. His rivals lacked Gluck's experience and dramatic insight. Confronted with an audience which expected excitement, and dramatic sense as well as musical beauty, Piccinni and Sacchini modified their styles but only occasionally matched Gluck's poignancy and force. Beside them Gluck was undoubtedly crude, but in the theatre abrasiveness can be an asset.

It is noteworthy that while some operas were still given first at Versailles, success or failure was now determined in Paris by an audience of mixed composition, ready to be swayed by intelligent argument. Gluck's supporters, such as the Abbé Arnaud and J. B. Suard, conscious of their champion's strength, were less shrill than the Piccinnistes and appealed more to the intellect of their readers. Audiences perceived the musical talents of the Italians, but were moved by the situations and personalities of Gluck's dramas. One wrote to the *Journal de Paris* to protest at a reviewer's condemnation of the intervention of the goddess Diana at the end of *Iphigénie en Tauride*: 'the unfortunate Orestes so intrigues me that I could not leave the theatre in fear of a return of these seizures which I had witnessed there . . . . nothing less than the goddess could assure my peace of mind'. Intelligent criticism need not reject miracles; the goddess was actually inserted into a second version of *Iphigénie en Aulide* in preference to the Racinian ending in which it is left uncertain whether a miracle has occurred. There is no hint of the capriciousness of Euripides' gods, although his plays were the source of many of these operas.

The Neoclassical values of the art of the French Revolution were apparent in the painting of J. L. David in the 1780s, notably the *Oath of the Horatii* (1785; the subject was used for a Salieri opera in Paris the following year, and one by Cimarosa in 1796). David presents a violent image of self-sacrificing patriotism, to which, in *Brutus* (1789), is added republicanism. Not only idealism, but the suffering it must entail, are contained in these powerful images, as they are in Gluck's direct portrayal of the Greek army on Aulis, like the barbarians of Tauris, clamouring for blood; a savage unison chorus, in which the fate of Troy is foreshadowed, makes the happy ending fragile. Gluck's music, here rough and violent, remained no less capable of poignancy, as in the aria added to *Alceste* ('Non ce n'est point un sacrifice'), or the heroine's role in *Armide*. Gluck orchestrated simply and tellingly (it is curious that he was criticized for noisy orchestration, to which Piccinni was far more prone). Gluck's dramatic intelligence is nowhere clearer than in his pacing of

18 J. L. David, *Oath of the Horatii* (1785). Values of selfless patriotism ascribed to ancient Rome are embodied in this early work by the master of official Neoclassicism under the French Revolution.

an opera; he resists the temptation of over-emphasis and builds scenes gradually towards a climax or an emotional release. When Armide intends to kill the sleeping Renaud, but finds she cannot, Gluck's music suffices to make clear her unconscious love of her enemy. In a masterpiece of narration in Act I of *Tauride*, Iphigenia's dream, violent events do not bring continual orchestral uproar; tension is controlled and anxieties gathered into a poignant aria.

Perhaps the most far-reaching element of Gluck's 'reform' is the individuality of each of his late operas. He adapts his musical ideas to the conditions of the drama, rather than forcing the drama to conform to a preconceived musical pattern. The mature Iphigenia of *Tauride* sings more broadly than her young self in *Aulide*; in the earlier opera her simple forms contrast with the complex utterances of Agamemnon, the protagonist for two acts and one of Gluck's finest character studies. Gluck was indebted to French models but no more adapted their conventions than he retained those of *opera seria*. He abandoned his own new monumentality in favour of flexibility and continuity; and the balance of solo, chorus, ensemble, recitative and dance, is reconsidered freshly for each opera. This conception of the uniqueness of an opera, quickly grasped by Mozart, is Gluck's bequest to Romanticism.

Nevertheless convention-oriented opera remained very much alive. No society as complacent as the late eighteenth century requires for its entertainment a continual series of artistic challenges. Working within the conventions, most composers took no risks with their audience. Although many works were affected by Gluck's ideas, he complained in the preface to *Paride* of not being imitated; his achievement in Vienna was localized although, unusually for Italian operas, his works were published in full scores. In Paris he effected a general revision of structure and musical style at the Opéra, but *opéra comique* needed no reform and modern instrumental music, to which Gluck contributed nothing, was already the fashion. By the time of his greatest triumphs Gluck was almost outmoded. If he founded no school, however, he left opera in a healthy state of flux; composers in the right circumstances could at least experiment in the knowledge that dramatic opera was a possibility.

The glittering and cultured court of Gustave III of Sweden, whose assassination at a masked ball in 1792 made him the hero of operas by Auber and Verdi, included a resident Mannheim-trained composer, Joseph Martin Kraus. The Swedish court opera theatre at Drottningholm survives in its original condition, and sets exist for *Iphigénie en Aulide* which, given in Swedish in 1778, formed part of a wholesale importation of the French Opéra repertory. Kraus was admired by both Gluck and Haydn; like some German operas, his Swedish version of the Dido story (*Aeneas i Carthago*) shows affinities to Gluck seldom found in the work of Italian composers.

The masterpiece of this type of opera is *Idomeneo, rè di Creta*, written for Munich in 1781 by Kraus's exact contemporary Mozart. *Idomeneo* derives from the French-influenced *opera seria* of Jommelli and Traetta, as well as from Gluck and Piccinni (Mozart saw *Roland* in Paris in 1778). It also owes much to the Mannheim orchestra, now resident in Munich. Gluck's impact is apparent in its conciseness of structure at critical points, notably those involving the chorus;

Mozart avoided elegance where it would detract from dramatic force. The scenes with the priests and the oracle are obviously indebted to *Alceste*. But Mozart also departs from Gluck by cultivating pure music. His arias, even the most intense, are longer and more gratifying to the voice; Mozart conforms to the expressive conventions and the limitations of the singers, while still enhancing the drama and characterization. The title role and the heroine Ilia are particularly well served. The stiff persons of the old French libretto, revised in Italian by a Salzburg Abbé of minor literary ability, become as nearly human as possible through the warming breath of Mozart's music (ill. 36).

Idomeneo is the supreme example of reformist *opera seria*, not only in musical quality but in harmonizing the libretto (which had a brutal tragic ending) to the spirit of the Enlightenment. The gods are not arbitrarily cruel – at least not to the ruling classes; only humble folk are killed by Neptune's monster – and divine intervention supports the institution of benevolent despotism, passing kingship to a new generation while reconciling enemies in the marriage of Idamante, the new king, to Ilia, the Trojan princess, rather than the Greek Electra. Electra departs with a recitative, and in one version an aria, of such explosive fury that she clearly represents the forces of demonic irrationality that the Enlightenment sought to expel. Undoubtedly Mozart could have redeemed serious opera, and he wished to do so. He revised *Idomeneo* in 1786 for a private performance, eliminating the castrato role (Idamante); and in the years of his greatest comedies he still angled for *seria* commissions. Finally, in 1791, he composed an opera for the coronation of the Emperor Leopold as King of Bohemia. As an example of imperial insensitivity Joseph II's verdict on *Die Entführung* pales beside the new Empress's comment; she called *La clemenza di Tito* 'German pigswill'. Nevertheless it was widely performed over the next twenty-five years, and was the first Mozart opera to reach London (in 1806).

In *La clemenza* Mozart returned perforce to the theme of benevolent kingship, and to Metastasio's justly popular libretto, 'trimmed', as Mozart put it, 'into a proper opera by Caterino Mazzolà'. A few complexities of plot were omitted, as were several arias; those that remain are mostly short, and some ensembles were added as well as a dramatic finale to Act I. Despite the presence of several castrati, Mozart managed to humanize his characters by

19 The Mozart family, *c.* 1780, by J. N. della Croce. The deceased mother is included as a portrait. The intensity of Wolfgang's expression contrasts with that of his sister.

adopting an idiom in which display is tempered, the instrumentation is lightened, and the minor characters, who in some operas (including *Idomeneo*) are granted the showiest arias, sing with unaffected simplicity. *La clemenza* was written in great haste, but so were most operas of the time; it coincided with the ever-popular *Magic Flute*, and it has been assumed that Mozart dashed it off without much thought, assigning the simple recitatives to his assistant Süssmayr. Only the last point is fair; doubtless Mozart would have replaced these inadequate recitatives had he lived. But much of the music achieves a rarefied beauty hinted at in parts of *Così fan tutte* and fully in keeping with Mozart's late style.

Nevertheless Mozart is at his greatest, and his most serious, in the three comedies written with Lorenzo da Ponte, and in *The Magic Flute*, which has the structure of pantomime. His achievement in *Le nozze di Figaro* (1786) is the more astonishing in that his previous experience in comedy had been patchy. An early *opera buffa*, *La finta semplice* (1768), shows a mature talent, but genius only in that it was written by a child. The best that can be said of *La finta giardiniera* (1775) is that it vies with the semi-serious operas of Haydn, musically rewarding but theatrically cumbersome. Mozart obeyed the conventions with the utmost conviction, yet hardly reached the same level as he already had in serious opera with *Lucio Silla*. Various comic projects aborted about 1783, one a collaboration with da Ponte. With *Der Schauspieldirektor* (*The Impresario*) Mozart contributed to the genre of satire on opera itself; but by then, early in 1786, he and da Ponte were at work on *Figaro*. In this they were stimulated by Paisiello's transformation of Beaumarchais' less complex *Le barbier de Séville* into an *opera buffa*, and also by the ban placed on *Le mariage de Figaro* in Vienna. Da Ponte claimed to have negotiated in person with the Emperor the approval of the subject for operatic purposes. But while he emphasized the sexual, rather than socio-political, motivation of the plot, the underlying message must have been clear to those acquainted with the play (which was available in print).

Lorenzo da Ponte was born into a Jewish family converted to Catholicism, and was destined for the church; but he had no vocation for celibacy. His tangled affairs, amorous and financial, led to his being forced to leave Venice; like Calzabigi twenty years before, he found refuge in Imperial Vienna, where he won the toleration of Joseph II and collaborated successfully with Salieri and Martín y Soler as well as Mozart. He was later to marry, despite being an abbé, and after a period in London he died in 1838, aged eighty-nine, as a citizen of the New World. His literary gifts were superior to most librettists', and his experiences gave his intrigues a verisimilitude enhanced by the ingenuity of his language. He was a magpie, taking more plots from others than he ever invented; two of his most successful works, *Figaro* and *Axur*, were translated from Beaumarchais, much of *Don Giovanni* is brilliantly adapted and improved from a libretto by Bertati, and the subject of *Così*, often considered original or based on a real-life incident, is the trial of lovers which has formed part of the common stock of European literary fantasy since the Middle Ages.

Mozart came to *Figaro* at the height of his powers, and burning to compose again for the theatre. His dramatic impulse already informed his instrumental music, notably the nine piano concertos written in 1784–5 (three more followed in 1786). The spirit of comic intrigue bubbles up in the coda to the variation finale of the G major concerto (κ453), and that of tragedy, or *Sturm und Drang*, informs the concerto most admired in the nineteenth century, the D minor (K466). The release of this pent-up invention could not have been more perfectly controlled than by an operatic version of Beaumarchais' very recent play (1784).

Mozart's comedies are inexhaustible sources of delight, and also debate as to their structure, their dramatic meaning, their wider significance, and their connection with the events of his life. It is sometimes suggested that they alienated the Viennese; but Mozart did not deliberately offend by any overt revolutionary proclamation; nor did the alleged licentiousness and social criticism in his operas bring about the decline in his fortunes which set in from about 1788, when *Don Giovanni* was performed in Vienna. When he died Mozart's prospects were improving and the financial embarrassments so well documented in his letters were not fundamental. It is sentimental to suppose that his early death was hastened by neglect and misunderstanding. His income was erratic, and it has been alleged that it was not well managed. But what primarily told against him was an economic system with little space for the freelance; the fees available for opera, for example, which took weeks or even months of work, were no substitute for a regular income. The patronage system, moreover, paid by reputation; when Mozart succeeded Gluck as Imperial Kammermusikus in 1787 it was at half the salary. Today he would have grown rich on the royalties of *Die Entführung* and *Don Giovanni*.

Mozart was no subversive, and he was supported by Joseph II who for all his enlightened ideas was severe on real sedition. There is admittedly a calculated ambiguity in *Figaro* and *Don Giovanni*, but both operas can be taken at their face value, as complex human documents. Mozart's greatest achievement was to inherit types from a long tradition of *opera buffa*, and to turn them into people as real as Shakespeare's, even if they express themselves through the international musical language of the age. Mozart could take the simplest of formulae and – by timing, by concentrated development of an idea, by some telling comment from the orchestra, by harmonic enrichment which might pass unnoticed in an instrumental work but which acquires significance through its pointed use in a particular dramatic situation, or by underlining a particular word – he could create out of common clay an image of living, thinking humanity.

20 Cherubino discovered by the Count, to the consternation of Susanna. The scene corresponds to the Trio in Act I of Mozart's *Figaro*, although here it illustrates Beaumarchais' play.

Figaro, for many people, is not only the first but the greatest Mozart/da Ponte opera. But the three are so unalike (despite the debt of *Don Giovanni* to *Figaro*) that distinctions of value are pointless. *Don Giovanni* has wholly serious characters and a supernatural element which Mozart handled with unparalleled power; *Così* is of unsurpassed musical loveliness; *Figaro* has the most vivid characters and the most ingenious plot, as well as the most direct social comment.

In structure these operas follow the lines laid down by Goldoni. The plot is mainly unfolded in recitative, but it continues to develop in ensembles and finales which consist of chains of ensembles. In ensembles the pace of dramatic movement is very variable. Some passages are as static as an aria; but *opera buffa* also develops action arias in which the stage is filled with business, like Figaro's 'Non più andrai'. Other passages in ensembles proceed at the pace of the action, like the Count's discovery of Cherubino hiding in a chair, in the masterly first-act trio. Part of the joke is that the trio is almost a quartet; although Cherubino is silent, Susanna and the audience know he is there. The Count's anger at the beginning refers to his memory of Cherubino's misdemeanours, and Basilio's unctuous phrase pretends to exonerate the boy; after the discovery the same music is used for the Count's expostulations and Basilio's malicious enjoyment of the situation. Thus the demands of musical form, in a varied recapitulation of motives, actually enhance the dramatic situation.

Figaro can be enjoyed as brilliant farce, its moments of gravity setting in relief the drunken gardener, the page's folly, the mistaken identities of the final act. It can also be analysed as social commentary, in which the jealousy of both Figaro and the Count smoulders with class hatred. What it can never be is simply a piece of wonderful music. It is that, of course, but the greatest of its musical attractions are stages in the plot whose seriousness and humour never conflict.

Figaro has a wholeness not shared by *Don Giovanni* and *Così*. But it would be wrong to credit the later comedies with no more than compensatory virtues, since their dramatic objectives would be falsified by any sense of wholeness. Don Giovanni's disappearance into Hell is followed by an epilogue which restores the tone of *opera buffa*, rudely shattered by the incursion of the walking statue. *Così* ends with the lovers united in their original pairings. Neither ending is as convincing as the end of *Figaro*. Admittedly we realize that the reconciliation of the Count and Rosina is fragile and will not last. But it does not matter; the reconciliation is part of the pattern of a long-term relationship, and the music suggests that when the Count falls again, he will again be forgiven. Cherubino will go to war; Susanna's virginity is reserved for her husband. An episode is closed, and an equilibrium achieved, within a perceptible human pattern such as cannot be imposed on the other operas.

In *Così* the original relationship between the pairs of lovers is bruised beyond repair by the events of the plot. The very heartlessness of the ending underlines the seriousness of what has happened within the opera, just as in *Don Giovanni* the very magnificence of the statue scene reduces the other characters to banality. These interpretations depend absolutely on the music. In *Così* da Ponte is heartless throughout and it is Mozart who makes his characters feel deeply,

21 The first known setting of the graveyard scene in Act II of *Don Giovanni*, by Joseph Quaglio (Mannheim, 1789).

while in *Don Giovanni* the finale demonstrates that the villain, the 'rake punished' of the full title, is also the hero; he has disrupted the others' lives but he has also vitalized them. To cut the finale of *Don Giovanni* (which may have happened as early in 1788, in Vienna) weakens the opera, even if its music lacks vigour until the actors step out of character and sing the moral 'chorus', ironically with a strict fugal opening.

The strength of these operas, and of *The Magic Flute*, is that they can support contradictory interpretations. Is *Don Giovanni* a Catholic opera, a symbol of revolution with a hero at war with his class, or a celebration of sexuality? It may be all or none of these things; it will reflect the predispositions of its critics. Its essence is as elusive as the quicksilver Giovanni himself, perpetually in motion, without a musical personality amidst the most solid characterizations of all opera; whether confronting an enemy, bullying a peasant, teasing his servant, or seducing, he is all mask and no substance. Into this vacuum has been poured a wealth of interpretation which would have astonished its creators, for Mozart and da Ponte believed not that they were producing a moral tract or an encoded revolutionary broadside, but that they were patching up a *dramma giocoso* out of another libretto with memories of Molière and some original action. The plot holds up under naturalistic analysis, but its origins are in the grisly farce of the fair theatres, not in Goldoni who rationalized the subject in a play. Mozart rose to the challenge by giving every detail the richest possible musical expression, whether in contrasting the three women, in the ludicrous antics of Leporello, or in the shattering apparition of the statue. The dance scene in the first finale, a *tour-de-force* in which three on-stage orchestras play tunes in different metres, was reckoned unplayable in Italy for over thirty years.

Even in the present century, when it began to be properly appreciated, *Così* has often been considered muted in comparison with its predecessors, and its plot undernourished. All too often it is played for farce, and appears trivial. Significantly, however, most of the farce is not audible in the music; Mozart, especially in the second act, took very seriously the consequences of a thoughtless bet (that the girls would not long resist the overtures of new lovers, actually the original ones in disguise). The utter improbability of the situation is a necessary condition for the exploration of feelings. It is futile to consider the work, as does Liebner, an illustration of frivolity on the brink of Vesuvius (revolution). There is no vestige of class conflict; Mozart is concerned with human weakness, which he views clearly and with compassion. The crux is the slow yielding of Fiordiligi to the blandishments of the disguised Ferrando, made impassioned after his betrayal by Dorabella. It is because Mozart, against the odds, actually makes something dramatic with this clever but otherwise unpromising text, that the ending seems arbitrary; we are invited to laugh off what has been shown to be no trifling matter. *Così* could be played as black comedy; it also approaches the style of *opera seria*, its symmetries of plot, its elaborate arias, its restricted cast, making an affectionate parody.

The Magic Flute belongs to a different world. Part pantomime, part ritual, a ragout of musical styles, naturalistic, supernatural, yet overtly ethical, it too mirrors its interpreters rather than yielding to explanation. Even today it is sometimes dismissed as a crude farrago of traditional comedy – was not Schikaneder, the librettist and first Papageno, a strolling player? – and propaganda – for were not he and Mozart both freemasons? Such views stop short of the work's essence.

22 The temples of Nature, Wisdom and Reason, with Sarastro; illustration for *The Magic Flute* (finale to Act I), dating from the era of the first production.

The origin of its elements can be traced, but that does not account for the miracle of their blending. It is not enough to treat the work as pure allegory. Perhaps the Queen of Night represents Maria Theresia, or the Catholic Church; Tamino, moving from blind belief in her to illumination and headship of the priestly order inimical to her, may be Joseph II, in which case Sarastro is the scientist and mason Ignaz von Born. But the allegory of Illuminist freemasonry is also one of human wholeness; sexuality is as important as in the da Ponte operas. Among other things *The Magic Flute* celebrates marriage. The depraved Monostatos desires Pamina out of lust; Papageno, child of nature, thinks of a wife and children; on a higher plane, woman is shown as man's equal, for it is Pamina who explains the mystery of the flute to Tamino before undergoing the ordeals of fire and water with him. The priestly order must cease its crude misogyny – a message freemasonry did not choose to hear. Attempts have been made, including one by Goethe, to write a sequel to *The Magic Flute*, but it is perfectly complete; wickedness is banished and superstition overcome by the rising sun of wisdom. It is perhaps the fullest artistic expression of the Enlightenment.

CHAPTER FIVE

Instrumental music: its uses, its resources, its meaning

Like the opera composer, the composer of instrumental music worked in a marketplace: to sell, he had to please. On the face of it this situation is not conducive to experiment, yet, for reasons both musical and sociological, instrumental music underwent a transformation during the late eighteenth century far more radical than that undergone by opera. Opera, at its inception, was the most innovatory of art-forms, but its move into the marketplace from the shelter of the courts forced conservatism upon it. Even Gluck's reforms developed over several years before attaining anything like a commercial value in France; and in many ways his French operas were conservative in relation to those written in Vienna. Public opera in Italy evolved by the gradual and inoffensive assimilation of 'reform' elements, *opéra comique* by the infiltration of elaborate music into the well-established framework of the play with songs. Notwithstanding major events like Gluck's arrival in Paris, change was gradual and did not significantly affect the general aesthetic of opera and its position in the various types of society in which it flourished.

On the surface, changes in instrumental music ran parallel to those in opera, just as the language of the symphony continued to be indebted to musical theatre. The transformation in instrumental music, however, involved a shift in aesthetic perspective too great to have been more than partly conditioned by the market. Undoubtedly a major factor was the growth of a large class of people who lived well above subsistence level but who did not suffer from the obligations imposed by membership of the old ruling classes. But it is far from certain whether the growth of the middle classes encouraged novelty in instrumental music, or whether composers, unconsciously in tune with other artistic movements, were moved to tease this market into accepting novelty. Despite the changes in instruments and instrumental forces, the surface of instrumental music altered hardly more than that of opera. But the consumer selecting among similar genre designations – sonata, concerto, fantasia, variations – by 1830, was buying something different in essence from what was available in 1750. Possibly the consumer of instrumental music was more open to adventure than the opera-goer, and throwing away what did not please would not preclude a further purchase. But composers of instrumental music were usually of a more innovative cast of mind than opera composers, and were moreover in more direct contact with the market, having no need of intermediaries, singers and impresarios. They usually performed both in private and in public; they presided over large-scale performances; they composed music for pupils and for a ready sale to amateurs. For composers to be both virtuosi and teachers was not new, and in this period of commercial expansion some added a new role, that of publisher. Despite political instability the rich pickings of the professional middle class became available to the musician; and the instrumental composer, once a provider of functional, didactic, and entertaining music, was freed from servitude and could become an artist with a message. In such a turmoil it is hardly possible to distinguish cause from effect.

Until well into the nineteenth century, much instrumental music continued to fulfil a definite, if ornamental, function. The Catholic Church still found a use for ensemble music in its services where local conditions allowed; Mozart wrote liturgical sonatas for Salzburg, and Good Friday at Cadiz in 1787 was celebrated with a series of orchestral meditations on the Seven Last Words, a masterpiece by Haydn. The organ remained the standard instrument for divine service, but organ music of the period is mostly conservative, and was not cultivated by major composers. In parts of Italy violins were regularly used to accompany the singing. In Burney's description of one church in Milan the instruments appear to dominate the proceedings:

. . . it was a Messa in Musica, by Signor Monza, and under his direction: his brother played the principal violoncello, with much facility of execution . . . the first violin was Signor Lucchini, who leads at the burletta; there were two or three *castrati* among the singers . . . the music was pretty; long and ingenious introductory symphonies to each *concerto*, as each part or division of the mass is sometimes called . . . [Lucchini] had several solo parts given him, and made three or four closes [cadenzas].

The music Burney heard at the convents on Sunday was a good deal simpler, and accompanied by organ and harpsichord. Even new church compositions retained a vestige of an older strict style including the improvised fugue and voluntary, but the *galant* instrumental style appeared in the operatic forms of many masses, motets and litanies.

At least in Catholic countries, therefore, the churches vied with opera houses and wealthy domestic establishments in employing musicians. The cultivation of instrumental music at court was crucial in the Baroque era and retained some importance even beyond 1800. Music was used for serious recreation; but Spohr's occasional indignation at privileged audiences for talking during his performance suggests that in general symphonies and concertos were listened to with attention. The talkers, however, may be excused when it is remembered that music also functioned as an element in the décor. As well as dance metres, domestic imitations of hunting or military music contributed to the language of table music (usually given its German designation *Tafelmusik*) or such recreational genres as Divertimento or Serenade. The principal condition of such music is that it should not demand to be listened to. It was prevailingly light, with Andante (walking speed) rather than Adagio (slow) movements contrasting with dances. Such works often come down in a pattern which it is tempting to standardize, such as moderate Allegro: Minuet: Andante: another Minuet: fast finale, perhaps a contredanse in rondo form. Table music was an excellent proving-ground; we owe Mozart's mastery of wind instruments to the needs of the Prince-Archbishop of Salzburg and those who commissioned divertimenti in Milan.

Background music was played by professionals; when the entertainment was meant to be listened to, the amateur would often take part. Frederick the Great at Sanssouci regaled his courtiers and guests with a nightly flute concerto, his own or one of three hundred by his teacher Quantz. Nikolaus I Esterházy played the baryton, a hybrid stringed instrument; for it Haydn wrote about 150 divertimenti, though not surprisingly these do not equal in interest works he was able to sell, such as string quartets. Frederick William, who became King of Prussia in 1786, was a cellist. He employed Boccherini as chamber composer, Haydn dedicated six quartets (op. 50) to him, and Mozart intended to do likewise; two of his last quartets are quite novel in texture because of their melodious cello parts. A commission, however, might be an act of disinterested patronage rather than a requirement for amateur performing material. Beethoven's 'Rasumovsky' and 'Galitzin' quartets were intended for performance by professionals, not princes. The merchant Tost, for whom Haydn wrote a dozen quartets and three symphonies, may have used music to his commercial advantage.

A musical education was socially acceptable among the minor aristocracy of Germany, who followed the example of their princes; the same cannot be said of Bourbon France or Hanoverian England. In his travels in Germany Burney frequently remarks on the musical accomplishments of distinguished persons, who were often competent and imaginative composers. Many of them were women, whom etiquette would not permit to appear in public or in print. In the middle strata of society women were less likely to be in the forefront except where they were indispensable, as singers (yet castrati continued to appear in opera into the nineteenth century). Occasionally featured as instrumental soloists or composers, women were not permitted among the musical rank and file. The best, however, were outstanding; for Therese Jansen Haydn wrote his three last sonatas and his late piano trios, which contain his most difficult keyboard music.

It was quite normal at this time for professional and amateur musicians to mingle, and for professional status to be a part-time affair. The Concert des Amateurs in Paris (later the Concert de la Loge Olympique, for which Haydn wrote his 'Paris' symphonies) was under the direction of composers such as Gossec, Simon le Duc, and the Chevalier de St Georges. The Viennese symphonist Karl von Ordonez played in the Imperial chamber orchestra, but was also a civil servant. The religious houses of Austria are a treasure-trove of copies of symphonies by Haydn and others, suggesting that monastic discipline may have included musical technique. In London, noble amateurs were involved in the foundation of societies such as the Concert of Ancient Music. It was only in the nineteenth century that amateur and professional standards again divided. Such organizations as the Philharmonic Society in London, or the Société des Concerts du Conservatoire in Paris, were dependent upon aristocratic or state funding, but were essentially professional organizations. The rise of virtuosi, and the changing aesthetic of serious instrumental music, led to much of it being beyond the skill of amateurs, and may have contributed to the maintaining of older music in the repertory (a significant phenomenon already in the nineteenth century) simply because it was easier.

The most important amateurs historically are the unknowns who bought music to play in privacy. On them depended the economic viability of music publishing. They bought light pieces, pieces which reminded them of concert and operatic music, including transcriptions, and variations on well-known tunes; but they also bought more complex music which served as a vehicle for self-communication through their instrument. It is this last class of buyer who sustained a change in the nature of music itself, and who formed the modern concert audience which expects from music not only delectation but emotional uplift.

One result of this growing market is that, instead of a few unreliable manuscript copies, music begins to survive in numerous early printed editions, often equally unreliable. 'Publication' includes professional copying by hand as well as engraving on plates; the expense of engraving would only be undertaken when a sale was virtually guaranteed. Copying provided a modest income, which sustained Rousseau in periods of difficulty, but it is not a safe way of transmitting music to posterity, and many works survive in our knowledge only by the appearance of *incipits* in Breitkopf's massive series of catalogues published from 1760 to 1787.

23 A page from Breitkopf's periodical catalogue. The first six incipits are Haydn's symphonies 75, 63, 70, 71, 62 and 74, all completed by *c.* 1780; the last is no. 73 (*La chasse*); the remainder are overtures including *Il ritorno di Tobia* (no. 6).

Another effect of the new public's buying-power was upon instrument manufacture. In the nineteenth century the piano became a status-symbol which in wealthy countries like Britain penetrated into the lower socio-economic groups. Already in the eighteenth century a remarkable number of relatively modest establishments could afford a keyboard instrument, usually a cembalo (harpsichord) or a pianoforte. Although this is not a period of great names in violin-making, new instruments were constantly required; old ones were treasured, and altered to suit modern techniques. Wind instruments suffered more rapid obsolescence because of technical advances such as new keywork to assist tuning or playing in unusual keys. Technical exploration continued in order to increase the range of notes available to trumpets and horns. Pistons were not widely used until after 1830, and horn-players developed skill in hand-stopping to fill in gaps between available notes. Both Haydn and Hummel wrote concertos for a short-lived chromatic trumpet with keys.

Instrumental developments ran parallel with new kinds of ensemble. Despite many colourful exceptions, the Baroque orchestra consisted mainly of strings and continuo. The Classical orchestra had a regular body of wind instruments, and the continuo, no longer texturally necessary, is reduced to being a seat for the director of the performance. Haydn presided over his 'London' symphonies at the piano, but it is doubtful if he played much, still less improvised during the performance; otherwise one of his jokes, the splutter of keyboard music near the end of Symphony no. 98, would have no point. An alternative method of direction was by the first violin – the 'leader' – and from this derived the method of beating time with rolled-up paper (not a new idea, ill. 7), a violin bow, or a stick, the modern baton. From a quasi-feudal band of servants the orchestra developed into a team of professional technicians with middle-class aspirations. The director controlled the performance in a dictatorial manner; the origins of modern conducting lie here, in the practices of Weber, Spohr, Spontini and Habeneck, who founded the Paris Société des Concerts on a repertory of Beethoven.

The orchestra was still based on string tone. Groupings like the Baroque trio or the French five-part texture began to die out. Some of Stamitz's symphonies are orchestral trios and Mozart occasionally uses divided violas, possibly expecting only one to a part; a multiple string quartet, with double basses (simplifying their parts if necessary), added to the cellos, became standard by about 1770. Musical architecture, as well as rhythmic definition and a firm texture, was increasingly affected by the use of wind. The standard group was two oboes and two horns, but the presence of a bassoon is usually to be inferred, doubling the cellos. Trumpets and drums were added in festal mood; oboists might take up flutes or clarinets in a slow movement. Only after 1780 did it become standard to include two or three families of high woodwind. Specialization developed in cities and opera orchestras in particular; at princely establishments in Germany players are known to have been engaged as, for example, violin and trumpet, taking up the latter as necessary (and thus reducing the strings). The restrictions on available notes for trumpets and horns ensure that their parts closely reflect the harmonic structure of the music, since they can only play in the tonic or closely-related keys. Similarly woodwind, until their mechanisms developed more sophistication, would be rested or lightly handled in tonally remote passages or for whole slow movements. The shock and exhilaration of the appearance of trumpets and drums in some slow movements in Haydn's London symphonies is difficult to recapture, as is the startling effect of these instruments apparently reinforcing the wrong key in the first movement of Beethoven's Ninth (the tonic D: the other instruments are cadencing in B flat). It is characteristic of the most imaginative composers that they could turn the apparent deficiencies of instruments to architectural or dramatic advantage.

Eighteenth-century orchestras varied greatly in size, some being little more than chamber groups: certain theatre pits had room for only twenty players or less. The attraction of mass effects and crescendo is generally associated with Mannheim but was also developed in the orchestras of larger cities. 'Double orchestras' were used by Gluck, J. C. Bach and Mozart. The latter, usually confined by circumstances to a small orchestra, was delighted by the size and skill of the Parisian forces and scored his *Paris* Symphony (no. 31 in D) accordingly. Eventually, increased string groups led to doubling the wind parts, and to the use of four horns; but while we know that composers liked the sonority and security of a large ensemble, most performances probably took place with fewer players than the ideal.

Variation in the standard ensemble might arise from circumstances, like the visiting players of whom Haydn took advantage in Symphony no. 31 (the *Horn Signal*). The clarinet became a normal

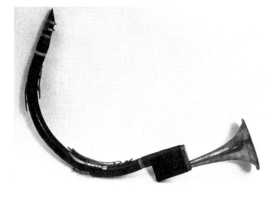

24 Basset-horn by Mayrhofer (Passau, c. 1770), an early example of this favoured domestic wind instrument, curved for ease of fingering.

member of the orchestra only in the 1790s; although it appears in music by Handel and Rameau, its availability was restricted. The few specialist players were featured in a considerable concerto literature and occasional use in theatre music, but the clarinet was also used in military wind bands made up of relatively unskilled musicians.

Gluck's orchestra for *Orfeo* (1762) includes cornetts, by then almost extinct; chalumeau, a single-reed instrument related to, but not a forbear of, the clarinet; and trombones. With *Alceste* (1767) Gluck produced the first modern orchestral *tutti*, including all woodwind families, trumpets, horns, trombones and strings. This effect of mass was emulated in Paris and elsewhere, but trombones continued for a few years to be used mainly for ritualistic scenes, to double choral parts, or to evoke the supernatural; in *Idomeneo* and *Don Giovanni* they appear only in one scene. Their use is extended in *The Magic Flute* and Beethoven brought them into his Fifth and Ninth symphonies to swell the orchestra for the finale; in Schubert's last symphonies they become full participants.

The wind were further varied by occasional use of small and large cousins such as the cor anglais (an alto oboe). Two are used in Haydn's Symphony no. 22 and in the divertimenti Mozart wrote for Salzburg, where there were no clarinets. The cor anglais forms the bass to an oboe trio in two works by Beethoven, but it was little used until the Romantic imagination found its peculiar tone-quality haunting and evocative, as in Berlioz's *Eight Scenes from Faust* (1829). The equivalent member of the clarinet family is the basset-horn, whose heyday coincided with the decline of the cor anglais. Mozart found it useful in chamber and orchestral groups including the great Serenade K361 for two oboes, two clarinets, two basset-horns, two bassoons,

82

four horns and string bass. It too had ritual and funereal associations, and appears in *The Magic Flute* and Mozart's Requiem. The piccolo, as a penetrating band instrument, is used to imitate birdsong, and for the whistling ploughman in Haydn's *The Seasons*. At the other extremity is the double bassoon; both enter the symphony orchestra, to amplify its range and sonority rather than vary its palette, in Beethoven's Fifth and Ninth symphonies. The double bassoon was an intractable bass for a wind group ('Harmonie'), as was the alternative favoured in France, the serpent, whose uncertainty of intonation prevented it ever establishing itself in the orchestra. A newly developed brass bass, the ophicleide, is featured in Mendelssohn's overture *A Midsummer Night's Dream* (1826).

The main development with smaller instrumental groups, notably the string quartet, was to dispense with the keyboard or to write its part out in full, not as a continuo but as a soloist or equal partner with a group of instruments, as in Mozart's innovatory quintet with wind and quartets with strings. The piano was increasingly the dominant keyboard instrument, and the harpsichord was in decline from about 1770, although in large spaces including opera houses it had the penetration and crispness needed to maintain orchestral ensemble and accompany simple recitative. Thanks to the conservatism of operatic styles, it survived longer in Italy than elsewhere, and a spinet was the first instrument used by Verdi. Such changes are more than matters of fashion, and effect the inner essence of music. The types of extended sonata movement most characteristic of the turn of the century arise in part from the potentialities of a keyboard capable of dynamic nuance, an orchestra of varying timbre, and a chamber group of equal partners.

Undoubtedly the single most important development was that of the 'cembalo col pian'e forte', which originated in the Florentine workshop of Cristofori around 1700. It used the body of a harpsichord, so that the first pianos were of the 'wing', 'harp', or small grand form. Instead of jacks plucking the strings, Cristofori inserted hammers to strike them, in essence a simpler mechanism with the advantage that relative loudness can be controlled by the player (hence the names, used indiscriminately, 'pianoforte' and 'fortepiano'). Cristofori's instruments were described in print, and were known to D. Scarlatti in Madrid. Further experiments were made in the 1730s by the German organ-maker Silbermann, some of whose

25 English double-manual harpsichord (*c.* 1768) by Jacob Kirckman, with lid-swell, perhaps intended to rival the dynamic variation of the piano.

26 Fortepiano (*c.* 1785) by a pupil of J. A. Stein of Augsburg, who was Mozart's preferred piano-maker.

27 Square piano by Muzio Clementi (London, *c.* 1812) with sustaining pedal, the ideal domestic instrument.

instruments, in the possession of Frederick the Great, were used by C. P. E. Bach and approved by J. S. Bach on his visit to Potsdam in 1747. In the next generation the divergent Austrian and Franco-British schools of piano-making predominated. The latter, by means of more elaborate actions and sturdier stringing, as well as of sheer size, developed greater power and versatility, and became the favourite instrument of travelling virtuosi from the 1790s. It was a period rich in experiment; the table-like square piano, derived perhaps from a clavichord, became a popular domestic instrument, and upright format was attempted by setting a grand piano on end, the so-called 'giraffe' piano. In emulation, harpsichord manufacturers such as Kirckman and Shudi developed the range and size of their instruments and incorporated a 'swell' device as well as stops which modified the tone. Stops appeared on pianos, including such bizarre effects as 'bassoon' and 'Turkish' (drum and cymbal) stops. More useful, and retained on all pianos today, were muting devices ('una corda' among others) and the capacity to raise the dampers and produce an 'open' or sustaining effect even when the keys are released; this operation was performed most efficiently by the knee or else, as today, by a pedal.

The two instruments coexisted for many years, set in harmonious rivalry in C. P. E. Bach's double concerto for piano and harpsichord. Much keyboard music is effective on both; the line is indistinctly drawn somewhere between Scarlatti and Beethoven. C. P. E. Bach

84

favoured the clavichord, a small-toned instrument capable of dynamic nuance, also enlarged during this period but destined to remain domestic. Publishers, mindful of the need to sell wherever possible, refrained from including directions such as dynamic nuance or pedalling which would preclude performance on the older instrument; it should never be assumed that music with dynamic markings is only fit for the piano, or music without them for the harpsichord. The earliest of Haydn's sonatas are 'divertimenti for cembalo' and the last were written for the splendid English piano of the 1790s, but most belong to the legitimate repertory of both instruments. We may well consider Mozart the first composer of great music for the pianoforte, but it is only in Beethoven's time that performance on the harpsichord becomes inadmissible.

Modifications of function in instrumental music and modifications of the means of its realization, the instruments themselves, must be viewed in the light of a modified understanding of its significance. In the mid-eighteenth century the prevailing aesthetic was that of the rationalist philosophers of the *Encyclopédie* who considered independent instrumental music to be fundamentally senseless: 'Music that portrays nothing is merely noise'. Instruments were classified by their extra-musical associations; the oboe was bucolic, the flute pathetic, the horn was for hunting, the trumpet was martial. Such associations found support in operatic music, especially in

France. Therefore, said d'Alembert, a flute concerto is an absurdity, since the instrument of mourning cannot decently indulge in passage-work. Needless to say composers were indifferent to such perversions of logic, and went on writing concertos for flute with no aim other than to appeal to the senses. The rationalist view of instrumental music is epitomized in Fontenelle's famous question, 'Sonate, que me veux-tu?' ('Sonata, what do you want of me?' or, more freely, 'what are you trying to tell me?'). If articulacy of thought is measured through language, music must remain inarticulate unless governed by words.

This philosophy was undermined by music which, unlike any sonata Fontenelle could have encountered, clearly has a communication to make, and is only inarticulate if it is insisted that thought is always verbal . The conception of non-verbal thought and expression is anathema to the rationalist; but long before the anti-rationalism of the Romantic movement, music began to be understood as having something to say to the receptive listener which could not be said in any other way. Already Rousseau allows the orchestra to tell us what the actor leaves unsaid (see above, p. 37). D'Alembert himself, while placing music below the literary and visual arts in importance, defined it in the preliminary discourse to the *Encyclopédie* as 'a kind of speech – even a language – by means of which the different feelings, or rather the different passions of the soul are expressed'. Honest writers would admit the independent expressive capacity of music, even if with qualifications, like Daniel Webb in 1769:

On hearing an overture by Jommelli or a concerto by Geminiani, we are in turn transported, exalted, delighted; the impetuous, the sublime, the tender take possession of the sense at the will of the composer.

He goes on, however, to say that 'eloquence' (meaning words) should 'cooperate with music and specify the motive of each particular impression'; the glimpse of independent expressiveness is vouchsafed only to be withdrawn. Others, such as Sulzer in his *Allgemeine Theorie* (*General Theory of the Fine Arts*), tried to specify the right means to express particular passions, thereby still restraining music to a system by which it can be decoded.

By the turn of the century the corner was turned, and music climbed the ladder of the arts, to reach the top rung in the philosophical scheme of Schopenhauer. As early as 1801 August Wilhelm von Schlegel, one of Germany's great intellectual polymaths, saw music as 'an image of our restless, mutable, ever-changing life', which is to recognize that sentience is not necessarily verbal. When E. T. A. Hoffmann (1776–1822) defined music as the romantic art *par excellence* he referred to the instrumental music of the late eighteenth century or founded therein, now (in 1810) reaching fulfilment in Beethoven:

Only instrumental music, which scorns all assistance from and combination with other art, can express with purity music's peculiar nature. It alone can give definition to the art. Music is the most romantic of all the arts; one might even say that it alone is purely romantic . . . . Music unlocks for man an unfamiliar world having nothing in common with the external material world . . . he forgets all feelings which he could define for another (in words), in order to surrender himself to the inexpressible.

For Schopenhauer, whose *World as Will and Representation* came out almost unnoticed in 1818, music is

a uniquely universal language, even exceeding in clarity that of the phenomenal world itself . . . the composer reveals the innermost essence of the world and expresses its deepest wisdom in a language that his reason does not understand.

Romanticism later embraced a blending of the arts – not only through collaboration, as in Wagner's 'Total work of art', but in interdependence, as in pictorially or literarily allusive ('programme') music, and in musically conceived poetry and even painting. Before that phase, however, 'Classical' instrumental music was understood as the purest and most spiritual form of human communication. Goethe wrote in 1829:

It is perhaps in music that the dignity of art is most eminently apparent, for music has no material element that has to be taken into account. It consists entirely of form and content; and it elevates and ennobles everything that it expresses.

The purest, non-verbal and non-representational forms represent musical essence; the orchestral symphony, rather than the opera, becomes the vehicle of a composer's highest aspirations. This priority, associated at first with Beethoven, has been challenged, but even today it is not entirely dethroned in the minds of composers, and certainly not in the mind of the concert-going public.

CHAPTER SIX

Keyboard music and the sonata principle

The obvious starting-point for a discussion of Classical instrumental music is composition for solo keyboard, where a transformation of style, coinciding with the tendency of divergent national styles to unite, is reflected in the rise of the pianoforte and the decline of the harpsichord. This reconciliation belongs to the generation of Bach's sons, but the most influential older master was Domenico Scarlatti (1685–1757). The brilliance, compactness and sophistication of his several hundred 'sonatas' (or 'lessons'), which were widely known through publication, challenged composers everywhere. His legacy in Spain, where his most distinctive follower was Antonio Soler (1729–83), did not endure. Instead Fernando Sor (1778–1839) succeeded in adapting the contemporary style in idiomatic sonatas and variations for guitar. With the Italian Giuliani (1781–1829), who also wrote guitar concertos, Sor was the leading figure in the brief Classical efflorescence of an instrument which, despite its cultivation by Paganini and occasional use by Weber, was neglected by major composers.

In England a Scarlatti cult was initiated by Roseingrave (1688–1766) and affected British keyboard composers such as Thomas Arne (1710–78) as well as J. C. Bach (1735–1832), who lived in London from 1762. Muzio Clementi (1752–1832) was brought up in England, forming another link between Italy and the 'London School' of keyboard music. Both England and France were mainly dependent upon foreigners in this field. After the decline of the French school of clavecinistes, nearly all significant keyboard composers in Paris for several years came from Germany. The most important were Schobert (c. 1735–67) and Eckardt (1735–1809); both were influenced by C. P. E. Bach and in turn affected the development of Mozart, who encountered their music in Paris as a boy. Travelling virtuosi like Steibelt, Dussek, and Clementi spent considerable periods in Paris, but the native contribution to piano literature (including works by Méhul and Boieldieu) was relatively small. Meanwhile the great keyboard tradition of Italy atrophied, although Galuppi made a great impression in Russia as a harpsichord virtuoso (from 1765 to 1768), and Domenico Paradies (1707–91) and Cimarosa wrote much attractive but musically lightweight keyboard music.

It is Germany and Austria which dominate the history of keyboard music and sonata forms; developments in other countries increasingly followed the example of the itinerant musicians of Germany, Austria and Bohemia, and of one at least who stayed at home. Known today as his father's son, Carl Philipp Emanuel Bach (1714–88) was the great Bach in his own time, and his keyboard playing, composition and teaching were more widely respected than his father's. Emanuel Bach could rise to the challenge of Scarlatti with a strong foundation in his native tradition, for keyboard playing occupied a central place in German musical life. Bach's achievement is embodied in sets of keyboard sonatas, with significant dedications: the 1742 set to his employer Frederick II, the 1744 set to his pupil Prince Karl Eugen, the 1760 set to a Princess of Prussia. But the six collections published between 1779 and 1787 are inscribed not to the nobility but 'Für Kenner und Liebhaber' ('for connoisseurs and amateurs'). Bach spent many years as Frederick's keyboard factotum; publication was intended, as with Haydn, to make his name known beyond the court circle. Eventually, in 1768, Bach followed the career-pattern of his father and his godfather Telemann by leaving royal employment for the service of a free city, Hamburg. There, despite being responsible for the music of a school and five churches, he found time to compile his testament of keyboard music and symphonies.

Emanuel Bach's most characteristic keyboard music is introspective, rather than brilliant like Scarlatti or monumental like his father's. His favoured keyboard techniques, such as the piano's 'open (sustaining) pedal' or the clavichord's vibrato ('Bebung'), are those which appeal subtly, drawing the listener into the composer's expressive world rather than exciting admiration. Bach is associated with the cultivation of sensibility ('Empfindsamkeit') and with the development of the Classical sonata style, and his earlier publications (including his treatise *Essay on the True Art of Playing the Keyboard*, which included six three-movement sonatas) had a profound and lasting influence. 'Sensibility' is reflected both on the surface and in structural elements of the music, whose fantastical nature derives from the mastery of improvisation to which Burney testifies. For the ornamental encrustation of Baroque and Rococo Bach substituted expressive ornamentation, with a freedom anticipating the rubato of Chopin. After the regularity of Baroque pulse, and contemporary with the symmetrical periods of operatic *galant*, Bach astonishes by the variety of pulse and note-values; he moves in bursts of activity and repose, often pausing on a harmony remote from the main key, to which he will then return with insouciance or pathos, according to the predominant mood. His fantasias contain harmonic excursions as recondite as their obvious model, his father's *Chromatic* Fantasia; his rondos take caprice to the point of indecorum.

Bach's influence, freely acknowledged by Haydn, resides mainly in his expansion of stylistic bounds and his seriousness, although his music does not lack novelty of form. Particularly significant was his inclusion within one movement of a multiplicity of contrasted ideas, often of very short duration. A flurry of different motives may introduce the key of the piece (or something that proves not to be the key of the piece, as in an F major sonata which begins in C minor). A new idea in sequence can bring about a modulation, yet more ideas will bring the section to a close. The outlines of sonata form ensure the possibility of coherence; in performance, only a sensitivity to mood coupled with a clear understanding of the form (and for preference an instrument of the period) will reproduce the almost hallucinatory experience which this music embodies.

SONATA FORM

At this point it is necessary to clarify what is meant by 'sonata form'. As a formal outline it refers, at least in the eighteenth century, to a binary movement, i.e. a movement in two parts, both clearly articulated by cadences and usually repeated: part 1, repeat, part 2, repeat (fig. 1). In most cases the cadences rhyme musically, but the first is in a different key from the movement as a whole. The most essential point is that part 1 moves to a second key; part 2 returns to the original key (tonic) and concludes by repeating in the tonic what was originally heard in the second key. One common pattern was that part 2 began with the material of the opening, in the second or yet another key; the tonic is then recovered using the music which originally defined the second key of part 1:

Fig. 1 Binary form

	part 1 (repeated)		part 2 (repeated)	
Keys	tonic	other	other(s)	tonic
Material	A	cadences	A	cadences

This design is common in Scarlatti and both C. P. E. and J. C. Bach. The two parts are of approximately equal length, whereas in binary dance forms (both Baroque, and the Classical Minuet) the second part is often twice as long as the first.

In a longer version of this form (fig. 2), part 1 (the 'exposition') corresponds to fig. 1. Part 2 has three crucial events. Its first section ('development') may or may not begin with the opening idea, but it has become a 'free fantasia' section, playing with any material from the exposition or introducing new ideas. The return of the tonic usually coincides with the return of the opening idea ('re-capitulation'), followed by cadences as in fig. 1. This section need not be a mechanical rearrangement of the exposition; Haydn is particularly good at keeping us guessing by shuffling the order of necessary events and introducing new developments.

Fig. 2 Sonata form

	part 1 (repeated) Exposition		part 2 (normally repeated) Development Recapitulation		
Keys	tonic	other	others	tonic	tonic
Material	A	cadences	various	A	cadences

Most eighteenth-century sonatas still require both parts to be repeated, but occasionally, and more frequently as movements grew longer, the second repeat is dropped; Beethoven hardly ever requires it. A noticeable division now arises within part 2 at the recovery of the tonic and the opening idea. When, early in the nineteenth century, the first repeat begins to be dropped (as in some of Beethoven's middle-period works), the original two-part model becomes the three-part model known to nineteenth-century theorists: exposition, development, recapitulation, to which a coda might be added. Nevertheless, the cadence to the exposition remains the strongest point of formal articulation and because it is in the 'wrong' key it marks the point of highest structural tension.

Nearly all contemporary accounts of Classical sonata form imply that the element defining the form is tonality, the underlying orientation by key centre. But the form is experienced through surface elements; the return of the home key is recognized, because it is greeted by a statement of ideas heard earlier. The thematic element is readily grasped, so that composers sometimes mark out the tonal areas by the introduction of new themes in the exposition's second key. But in the eighteenth century they were particularly resourceful in playing on underlying expectations of departure and return by disposing thematic ideas in different ways. The surface elements depend on an underlying structure; the latter is constant so that the former can be the subject of infinite, improvisatory variation.

C. P. E. Bach's capriciousness results from a love of discontinuity and surprise. Haydn, whose surprises result from a nervous sensibility as well as from his celebrated sense of humour, achieved a more stable balance between caprice and consequentiality. He often concentrates on very few ideas in the exposition, and is prone to subject the opening to immediate development. Many of his finest movements use an absolute minimum of thematic material. Both these composers tended to drive the music through the point when the exposition's second key is reached, so that we recognize it as established only when we also recognize closure; the prolonging of the cadences is among the greatest delights of the form. But Haydn often does what Mozart and Beethoven preferred, to bring the music to a clear point of punctuation and present the second key as clearly as the tonic by the introduction of a new theme or the restatement of the opening. The distinction between a two-theme and a 'monothematic' sonata movement is relatively unimportant; these are just two of several possible ploys. More important is to note that in a monothematic sonata movement (such as Mozart's late Piano Sonata in B flat K570, or Haydn's last symphony, no. 104 in D) the original theme is significantly altered when used to establish the second key.

The processes of sonata form are just as applicable to music for full orchestra as to works for one or two instruments designated 'sonatas'. A work for three instruments may be called 'Sonata' or

'Divertimento', but it may also be called 'Trio'; hence a String Quartet is a sonata for two violins, viola and cello, and Symphony is a sonata for orchestra. As a term for the whole composition, 'sonata' implies a multi-movement work (two to five movements), but not all of the movements will necessarily be in sonata form.

The origins of sonata form have been traced not only in the binary design described above, but also in the mid-century expanded aria (Rosen, *Sonata Forms*). But sonata form is one of the outlines employed by Stamitz in symphonies written about 1740, nearly a century before the form was codified. Sonata principles can be applied to many kinds of movement because sonata is not a formal blueprint; as Rosen puts it in *The Classical Style*, 'it is, like the fugue, a way of writing, a feeling for proportion, direction, and texture rather than a pattern'.

Other forms directly affected by the sonata include a two-part form, in effect a sonata without repeats or development, common in slow movements and overtures; and a rondo design, where a simple dance-like form (on the extendible pattern ABACA, etc.) is enriched by thematic development and the tonic reprise of B to form 'sonata-rondo'. Variation movements, which abounded throughout the 'Classical' period, may seem diametrically opposed to the overarching sonata principle in that they necessarily consist of discrete sections. Classical sets, however, frequently merge the final variation into a sonata-like development or peroration. Haydn devised a kind of movement which sets out like variations, only to develop and recapitulate like a sonata. A short but subtle example is the slow movement of the D minor quartet (op. 76 no. 2, the *Fifths*); its progeny includes magnificent works by Beethoven, among them the finales of the *Eroica* and Ninth Symphonies.

The *galant* style was partly a reaction against contrapuntal rigour (see Chapter 2), but fugue remained alive as a scholastic discipline and Haydn and Ordonez brought it into contact with the divertimento by introducing strict fugal movements into string quartets. Haydn wrote four fugal quartet finales; three in op. 20, but only one (op. 50 no. 4) after the full realization of his thematic style in op. 33. Mozart ended the first of his quartets dedicated to Haydn (к387 in G) with a fugue integrated into the design of a sonata; scholastic fugue defines the formal pillars (opening, second key, development, recapitulation) and the remaining material is *galant*, even ostentatiously lively.

93

When Schubert presents a secondary tonal area by means of a new theme with two variations (Piano Sonata in C minor, 1828), the incorporation of opposed principles into the sonata is completed. This, however, is an extreme instance of Schubert's tendency to extend sonatas by lyrical periods, which inevitably undermine the dramatic density of the Classical style. The post-Classical and Romantic sonata, with some exceptions, have essentially different underlying principles from the Classical type, superficial similarities notwithstanding. When they wrote sonatas, it was the Romantics who were formalists, and the Classics, because the apparent constraints were no more than the requirements of intelligibility, who were improvisors. In the maturity of Haydn and Mozart, and for a little time afterwards, the sonata principle was universal and hence an area for experiment. Its concealed background represented rationality and control, its foreground fantasy, this essence being reducible to an image of Enlightenment: ordered freedom.

Good principles do not guarantee fine music. A minor composer can make a sonata appear stiff and predictable. In the aural equivalent of a poor light the charming J. C. Bach can be mistaken for Mozart, but under close examination (or repeated hearing) he appears too symmetrical both in the deeper (structural) and surface (rhythmical and phraseological) aspects. A *galant* composer *par excellence*, J. C. Bach broke away from the family ambience to study in Italy, and his years in London were broken only to produce Italian operas in Mannheim and a single French opera. His keyboard sonatas, made of fluent allegros, gentle but seldom melancholic andantes, and brilliant finales, make a satisfying pattern without much intellectual depth, the perfect style for cultivated gentlefolk attracted to Italian opera. Exceptional is a grand sonata in C minor which begins with a weighty Adagio and a powerful double fugue; Bach was a loyal pupil of Padre Martini. Even here, however, he ends in *galant* vein, with a delightful gavotte. J. C. and C. P. E. Bach, both perhaps in reaction from their magisterial father, are at opposite ends of a spectrum; the younger man making a virtue of conventionality, the elder (J. C.'s first teacher) unquestionably quirky. If Haydn's early style is close to that of Sammartini, and Mozart's to that of J. C. Bach, C. P. E. Bach was the necessary counterpoise in the balance of convention and fantasy which makes a 'Classical style'.

It is usual to refer to the 'Viennese Classics', because Vienna was the final home of, indisputably, the three greatest masters. Rosen subtitles his *The Classical Style* simply 'Haydn, Mozart, Beethoven'. Neither of the Bachs, nor Schubert (for all that he really was Viennese), fit within the canonical boundaries, defined not by a composer attaining the status of a classic – which could hardly be denied to Schubert – but by the internal mechanism of the Classical style as revealed in a close study of both typical and unique features in individual compositions of Haydn, Mozart and Beethoven. There is, however, as much common ground between genius and talent in this as in any earlier era, and more than in the nineteenth century. Vienna was only one capital where the general attributes of 'Classical music' were cherished and where the complexities of Haydn, at least, were not only acceptable but actually popular. Most good composers were neither Viennese nor based in the Imperial capital. If the finest musical education was probably still to be had in Italy, the most musically educated population, in all walks of life, was Bohemian. Its population disrupted by the Seven Years' War (1756–63), Bohemia continued to furnish Europe with instrumentalists and instrumental composers as freely as Italy produced opera singers and composers: after Stamitz and the Benda family came Reicha in Bonn and Paris, Gyrowetz and Dussek everywhere, and in Vienna itself Vanhal, Kozeluch, Wranitzky and Krommer. But there were hosts of other instrumental composers with a similar technique and aesthetic: among the more individualized are Boccherini, Dittersdorf, Michael Haydn, Kraus, and later Hummel, Clementi and Spohr. In instrumental music the disparity between the three classics and the rest seems greater than in opera, where only Mozart stands out. Otherwise the minor composers in their quartets, symphonies, sonatas, concertos, suffer by seeming to imitate Haydn, or by having been surpassed in imitations by Mozart, or by dissipating in lyrical or virtuosic expansiveness tension which Beethoven, in similar movements, would have allowed to accumulate to maximum dramatic advantage. But so many of these works are more than competent that they deserve a corner of today's expanded repertory. In what follows it is hoped to represent the magnitude and variety of instrumental music without presenting a catalogue, and to do some justice to the general mass of composers while giving due prominence to the best.

CHAPTER SEVEN

The principal genres of instrumental music to c. 1800

It is natural to assume that the principal genres of instrumental music are those which predominate in our repertory. In fact, however, the supremacy of sonata movements for piano, string quartet or orchestra is as much a result of nineteenth-century preferences as those of the Classical period. Piano sonatas were in origin teaching rather than performance material; few string quartets had a permanent membership even when (after *c.* 1790) the medium appeared in public concerts. Only the orchestra was comparable to its present form, and orchestral concerts usually included far more works than they do today, with vocal and instrumental solos accompanied by piano forming a relish to the weightier compositions for the full ensemble.

The late eighteenth century was a period when composition and instrumental medium were not so inextricable in the composer's conception as they have since become. The genre of keyboard sonata accompanied by violin (usually, but also by cello or a wind instrument) was closely related to the piano sonata; in some works of Pleyel and Clementi the violin (or in trios both violin and cello) can be omitted with little damage. Mozart's violin sonatas encapsulate the history of the emancipation of the string part from accompaniment to a subordinate but obligatory role, and then to equal partnership (as in his last violin sonata K526). Beethoven picked up the genre from this point; his op. 5 sonatas are dedicated to the cellist, not the pianist. Nevertheless Haydn continued, in his marvellous late trios, to compose what are essentially keyboard works with accompaniment.

Transcription was also common, and in the hands of a master becomes high art. The string trio versions of three fine Haydn keyboard sonatas may not be authentic, but they are undeniably effective. Haydn himself arranged his *Seven Last Words* for string quartet (op. 51) and supervised a piano version; one of Haydn's ripest symphonic slow movements, that of no. 102 in B flat, serves also for the beautiful late piano trio in F sharp minor. A work that is ostensibly *Tafelmusik*, the impassioned Serenade in C minor for wind octet

28 Portrait of Joseph Haydn by George Dance (London, 20 March 1794); Haydn at 62 was at the height of his fame.

K388, was adapted by Mozart for string quintet, the medium of his most elaborate chamber music. Beethoven, partly under pressure to maintain a flow of publications, turned his quintet for piano and wind op. 16 into a quartet for piano and strings; his great piano trio op. 1 no. 3 appears as a string quintet op. 104; and the isolated string quartet in F of 1802 tried to forestall acts of piracy on a favourite piano sonata, op. 14 no. 1 in E. Transcription by publishers' hacks was all too common, and took on a popularizing aspect which may in the end have encouraged the sale of authentic versions. Operatic full scores, if published at all, were prohibitively expensive; the amateur could enjoy versions for piano, voice and piano, string quartet, or wind groups. The latter tradition is used by Mozart in the supper scene of *Don Giovanni*, where a wind octet ('Harmonie') plays *Tafelmusik* taken from operas recently heard in Prague; the third number is a humorously vulgarized version of his own 'Non più andrai' from *Figaro*.

Classification by title is a far from certain guide to the nature of the musical discourse. 'Divertimento' is used by Haydn for piano sonatas, trios, and all his quartets ('divertimenti a quattro') up to and including op. 20, and Mozart used it for the magnificent string trio κ563. Even 'concerto' is not unambiguous. Three Mozart concertos (κ413–15), scored for a standard orchestra, can be played with solo strings and no wind, but the resulting ensemble is not the true chamber 'piano quintet', since the pianist is soloist and continuo rather than an equal partner. Yet only a few months later Mozart began a series of piano concertos among whose glories is the obbligato wind writing. Haydn, in countenancing Pleyel's edition of his string quartets, not only included 'op. 3' which is believed to be by R. R. Hoffstetter, but within op. 1 and op. 2 included three early symphonies in spurious arrangements. The classification of such music, with composers as prolific as Haydn, Boccherini, or Pleyel, has been a major undertaking of modern musical scholarship.

The mutual involvement of different instrumental groupings should be seen as an enrichment of musical life rather than a cause of confusion. The idioms of different instruments continued, as in the Baroque, to fertilize each other, as did the textures of characteristic instrumental ensembles. The concerto and symphony were intimately related throughout the eighteenth century; the Baroque 'orchestral concerto' and 'concerto grosso' were recent phenomena. The multiple concerto enjoyed great popularity in the concert life of Paris especially, and it was normally given the mixed title of 'Symphonie concertante' (Sinfonia concertante). Mozart wrote such a work for four wind players from Mannheim, destined for the Paris Concert Spirituel; Haydn wrote one for London for mixed string and wind soloists; Pleyel wrote half-a-dozen using from two to seven soloists. The masterpieces of this genre are Mozart's Salzburg Sinfonia Concertante in E flat (κ364, for violin and viola), and Beethoven's Triple Concerto of c. 1804 (op. 56, for violin, cello and piano).

The symphonic nature of such works may seem diluted, but the use of solo instruments in symphonies is another indication of fruitful mixture of genres. The best-known and most original examples are by Haydn. There are many violin solos in his symphonies up to no. 98, where the impresario/leader's name 'Salomon' appears in the autograph score. Elaborate solos appear in several early symphonies including the *Horn Signal* (no. 31), which uses solo violin and cello in the slow movement; and with rather elephantine humour Haydn scored the trios of several minuets as solos for double bass.

When concertante elements were edged out of the increasingly intellectual – indeed, symphonic – symphony, symphonic dialectic entered the concerto. One of Mozart's inspired syntheses of fugue and sonata (in this case sonata-rondo) is the finale of the Piano Concerto in F, K459. Beethoven's last three piano concertos and his one violin concerto (which he also arranged for piano) vie with the symphonies among the most significant compositions of his heroic phase. The pervasive thematic working which is implied in the term 'symphonic' is actually best served, without distraction from heterogeneous timbres, by the string quartet and quintet; the former in particular has become symbolic of a conception of music as a complex conversation-piece, so that its post-Classical development diverges sharply from that of the piano sonata. Where Haydn called both quartet and sonata 'divertimento', transcription between these media is almost inconceivable a generation later, and impossible with late Beethoven and Schubert.

PIANO MUSIC

Returning to the piano to survey its vast literature requires no apology. The rapid development of the instrument itself went hand in hand with its idiom, so that throughout our period and beyond it remained at the forefront of what was undoubtedly considered the progress of the art.

The composers of piano music demonstrate the remarkable homogeneity of musical Europe, a condition of affairs not directly affected by the French Revolutionary and Napoleonic wars and only undermined by the consequent, but later, infiltration of nationalism into artistic affairs. The nearest approach to a cohesive group of composers, the 'London Pianoforte School', included Italian, German, Bohemian and Irish composers who also worked in France, Austria and Russia. In consequence even those who did not travel, like Mozart and Beethoven, had a wide range of models to assimilate and synthesize. Yet despite the background of homogeneity this was a period of individualists, piano virtuosi with their own tricks, or with a special relation to a maker of instruments, by which they hoped to put a personal stamp on their performance.

After the Bachs, Schobert, and Eckardt (who went with the Austrian piano-maker Stein to Paris), the first composer to conform to this pattern was Mozart himself; the next was the cosmopolitan, Clementi. When they met in Vienna in 1781 Clementi was immensely impressed by the 'spirit and grace' of his younger contemporary (who had preceded Clementi by performing all over Europe as a prodigy). Mozart was less generous. He sensed in Clementi a technician rather than an artist, brilliant in execution of scales in thirds, but 'without a kreutzer's worth of taste or feeling'. Mozart here reveals himself as the disciple of both the sons of Bach. With a strong Italian orientation, he gravitated naturally to J. C. Bach, but as he recognized the potential of the new instrument he developed his own response to 'Empfindsamkeit' and the intellectual brilliance of Haydn. Nevertheless his piano fantasias and sonatas, except perhaps the huge coupled Fantasia and Sonata in C minor K475 and K457, must soon have seemed old-fashioned to those acquainted with larger pianos than Mozart was able to use.

Mozart's concertos, however, marked the establishment of the Classical concerto as more than a work of virtuosity; and they survived the growth of the piano (and the parallel growth of the orchestra) because their musical ideas are not dependent on the limits of the instrument or the player's skill. In fact, in accordance with principles which can be inferred from Mozart's critique of Clementi, they subjugate an undoubted brilliance to taste and feeling. In these concertos the perfect balance is struck between solo and orchestra, a constructive partnership without rivalry, the light, penetrating tone of the Viennese piano set off by the strings or pitted against soloistic work from the wind. The woodwind writing in K482 in E flat and K491 in C minor is possibly the most elaborate in the eighteenth century, while the piano plays on a backcloth of string tone, often duplicating the principal voices in the midst of delicate figuration. These works are not, however, merely pretty. The D minor and C minor concertos have all the tragic power we associate with Beethoven in those keys. The graceful A major concerto K488 has an incomparable elegy for its slow movement, and the Andante of K467 in C is a sublimation of aria, a floating melody over gentle pulsations which takes us near to heaven. Brilliance and pathos, mercurial changes of mood, are tempered by a rigorous balance between the requirement that a concerto seem improvisatory and the need for formal discipline. This balance is struck not only in the complex sonata/ritornello forms used for opening movements, but in the variation sets (notably the finale of the C minor concerto), and the rondos with which the concertos usually finish.

Mozart wrote twelve concertos in the years 1784–6, some for pupils but mainly for his own 'Academies'. After the magnificent K503 in C he wrote only two more, the *Coronation* Concerto K537, a *pièce d'occasion*, and K595 in B flat, from the year of his death. It is probable that this change in orientation resulted from external circumstances; for whatever reason, he seems not to have promoted or appeared in concerts so often after 1786. The autumnal smoothness of K595 resembles Mozart's last concerto, for clarinet, but its joyous finale, based on a recent song welcoming the spring, suggests that the form was by no means exhausted. A number of these concertos were published, and some were in the repertory of pianists such as Hummel and Beethoven. It must soon have been widely recognized that they form a unique synthesis, after which the piano concerto was forced to divide itself between works of symphonic aspiration, notably the last three of Beethoven, or works of virtuosic brilliance with orchestral accompaniment, like those of Dussek and Field.

The concerto's three-movement form was almost invariable, but the sonata could take on many shapes. A high proportion before 1790 are in only two movements or deploy the three in more varied patterns than the concerto's fast—slow—fast. Mozart's only substantial work in E minor, the Violin Sonata K304, consists of an allegro and a minuet; the Violin Sonata in G K379 has a slow movement linked to an allegro in G minor, then a set of variations; the Piano Sonata in A K331 consists of variations, minuet, and rondo *alla turca*. One of Haydn's finest late sonatas (no. 48 in C) consists only of a set of variations of a favourite type, alternately in major and minor, and a brilliant rondo. The three-movement pattern was commoner, however, and with the addition of a minuet or scherzo the four-movement pattern of string quartet and symphony was increasingly followed. Beethoven is exceptional, in his later years, in designing several sonatas with only two movements: it was doubtless because op. 111 ends with a slow movement that, to the composer's annoyance, his publisher enquired whether the rest had gone missing.

The sonata was by no means the only common form of piano music. Besides the notated improvisations called 'fantasia' or 'capriccio', variations provided a framework for a brilliant technique, improvisatory fantasy and compositional skill. Mozart's variations, usually on popular operatic melodies, were his best-known piano works in the 1790s, when Beethoven began to contribute to this form. It may signify his low opinion of them that Beethoven usually published variations without an opus number, but two sets on his own themes were granted that accolade as opp. 34 and 35. With these he broke the bounds of straightforwardly consumable music and elevated the independent variation set to an artistic plane equivalent to the sonata, preparing the ground for his supreme achievement, and his last great piano work, the Diabelli Variations.

Mozart and Beethoven were virtuosi; but they were composers first. Others came to composition through the need to support their own virtuosity. One such was Daniel Steibelt (1765–1823), who composed sonatas and concertos but also immensely popular operatic potpourris and programmatic works, in which he exploited every resource of the instrument – pedals, tremolandi imitating orchestral strings, the recently extended treble and bass, and 'three-handed' techniques including the well-tried hand-crossing and the new technique, dependent on the sustaining pedal, of playing bass notes and middle-register accompaniments with an agile left hand. Steibelt's immense productivity was by no means exceptional; his style is short-winded and superficial, but he did much to establish the pattern of piano virtuosity based on immaculate technique and keyboard control, displayed to best advantage in small undivided forms which concentrate on particular technical problems. Antithetical to the sonata principle, such works are usually termed 'study' (étude), and the best present the player with as much of a poetic as a technical challenge.

Muzio Clementi (1752–1832) was brought to England as a boy by the eccentric Peter Beckford, who 'bought him of his father for seven years'. Having exchanged the harpsichord for the piano, he entered the concert life of London in his twenties before embarking on the continental tour which brought him face to face with Mozart. Clementi's impact on the development of serious music for piano was considerable, but his influence tended away from Classical intensity towards a looser architecture able to accommodate both operatic

29 Portrait of Muzio Clementi by
Thomas Hardy (*fl.* 1778–98).

sentiment and technical brilliance. The sonata became a concert piece.
Clementi's ideas were propagated by his teaching, travelling and
activity as one of the leading London publishers and piano
manufacturers; and his career blossomed, in contrast to the continual
difficulties which beset his closest rival, the Bohemian Jan Ladislav
Dussek (Dusík) (1760–1812). After private study, Dussek may have
worked with C. P. E. Bach in Hamburg (*c.* 1782). His nomadic career
included periods in Paris, London and Germany; he became a
publisher in London, in partnership with his father-in-law Corri, and
worked closely with Broadwood when he extended the range of the
piano to six octaves. Despite his business failure – he fled his creditors
in 1799 – Dussek was much sought after as performer and teacher; he
is also of importance in the development of the virtuoso piano
concerto, which Clementi surprisingly neglected.

The sonata style of Clementi and Dussek exemplifies what Rosen
has called the phase of 'Classicistic' instrumental music. By analogy
with 'Hellenistic', 'Classicistic' implies the extension, or inflation, of

Classical idioms without the intellectual tautness of the 'true' (Viennese) classics. The balance of formal precision and dramatic content is imperilled by a more leisured progress; in a sonata exposition tonally stable areas are expanded and the cadences develop into extended concerto-like figuration, yet there is no abbreviation of bridge-passages and development. Despite its looseness, this style has its own rewards, and it was where Beethoven began. His sonata in C op. 2 no. 3 is dedicated to Haydn, but its grandiose structure of four movements, with a cadenza in the first, feels more like a tribute to Clementi. Beethoven, however, in adapting the time-scale of the symphony and string quartet to the sonata, imbued it with the qualities of mass and density of thought found in his 'symphonic' quartets; in going, with Clementi, beyond Classicism, he did not lose touch with its spirit.

The constellation of the London Pianoforte School included, besides Clementi and Dussek, Clementi's pupil (and rival, as composer and publisher), Johann Baptist Cramer, from Mannheim (1771–1858); and a Frenchman of German parentage, Frederic Kalkbrenner (1785–1849), who had studied in Vienna with Haydn. Kalkbrenner was based in England only from 1814 to 1823. His later career as teacher and international virtuoso, centred on Paris, seems to have stifled a considerable compositional talent; his sonatas, works of high seriousness despite their difficulty, are mainly from his earlier years. One of the most remarkable talents of this generation was an Englishman. The small surviving corpus of keyboard and violin music by George Frederick Pinto (1785–1806) makes his early death particularly regrettable; his sonatas, stylistically close to Dussek, have a youth's flaws and extravagances, but their depth of feeling and imagination make comparison with Schubert by no means absurd.

Among Viennese composers Beethoven's principal rival was Johann Nepomuk Hummel (1778–1837). Hummel lived in Mozart's house as a boy; like Beethoven, he subsequently studied with the most celebrated Viennese teachers, Albrechtsberger for counterpoint and Salieri for vocal composition. Hummel held court posts at Esterház, Stuttgart and Weimar, which he combined with a performing career. His large output includes virtuoso works for solo piano and piano-dominated chamber music (such as the 'Military Septet' with trumpet), as well as concertos and rondos with orchestral accompaniment.

The sonatas of Hummel and Carl Maria von Weber (1786–1826) exemplify tendencies which may well be considered not so much Classicistic but anti-Classical. Material is normally so disposed as to proceed from a clear tonic statement to the second key, raising the musical temperature by acceleration of note-values, harmonic change, and turnover of thematic ideas. The opposite strategy is to begin with an ambiguous or violent gesture; the main tonality is withheld – Weber's C major sonata (1812) begins as if in D minor – and the music is already at boiling-point, as in the outer movements of Hummel's remarkable sonata in F sharp minor (1819). With the eventual move to the second key, the music relaxes into a lyrical outpouring, after which it is necessary to work up the temperature again in order to cadence decisively; this is usually done by allowing difficult figuration to proliferate, loosening the residual 'symphonic' element beyond recall. The slow movement of the same Hummel sonata is like an operatic *scena*, blending severe figures with lyricism encrusted in ornament. Both composers included four movements in their sonatas, the minuets and scherzos, as in early Beethoven, being particularly attractive.

Beethoven's personal synthesis of Classicistic breadth with Classic vigour, through its authority and intensity, seems to touch the preoccupations of Romanticism. An example is the F minor sonata op. 57 known as *Appassionata* (1804). The first movement has three thematic areas, a striking enrichment being the use of a minor key for the last. The intricate relation of thematic ideas and the pervading semitonal motif press the argument unrelentingly on, so that the structure is expansive without any hint of looseness. The movement culminates in a powerful coda. An additional section after the recapitulation, this feature, on which Beethoven increasingly depended for the fullest presentation of his ideas, erodes the symmetries of Classical form but does not subvert its essence. No less characteristic of Beethoven's middle period are bold schemes like the two sonatas headed 'Quasi una fantasia', op. 27, and the remarkably compact op. 54 in F which consists of an ornamental rondo in minuet style followed by a limpid *perpetuum mobile*. If the scheme sounds like a throwback to Haydn, Beethoven is exploring areas of sensibility uncharted by his former teacher.

In the *Waldstein* and *Appassionata* sonatas, and in the later *Les adieux* which makes music of a simple programmatic sequence (farewell, absence and return), Beethoven's command of a large-scale architecture which is also dramatically paced depends on his attention to all aspects of musical presentation, large and small. This command was won with difficulty, even by curbing his natural fluency. From his sketches it appears that Beethoven had a vision of a whole work, which he could sustain over years. He might have composed quickly but the result would not have met his exacting standards. Instead he worked towards his ideal conception by notating ideas in a crude form and reshaping them into the plastic themes which sound so spontaneous, drafting the plan of whole movements, working over details, and only then, and still with many changes of mind, writing out the entire score. Beethoven's sketches form one of the largest and most complex documentations of compositional process that we possess. It must not be supposed, however, that his working methods were any more typical than the compositions themselves.

CHAMBER MUSIC

No ensemble possesses a repertory to match the densely-argued masterpieces for string quartet. Nevertheless it should not be assumed that composers and consumers acknowledged its pre-eminence, at least before Beethoven. The 'divertimento a tre' (two violins and cello) is not a deficient string quartet but a Classical instrumental grouping; as in the Baroque, the basic chamber texture was of three parts, until Haydn's opp. 20 and 33 confirmed the value of a viola. Between 1750 and 1780 more trios than quartets were published, including many by Haydn. Of the two leading chamber composers, however, Joseph Haydn (1732–1809) finally favoured the quartet, and Luigi Boccherini (1743–1805) the quintet with two cellos. It was the tolerance of intellectuality which assisted the quartet to its present status; only Mozart, who adopted the darker-hued quintet with two violas, could exploit (rather than pointlessly resist) the seductive qualities of the larger ensemble without risk to musical architecture.

Boccherini's early music is delightful and varied, but his later works are disappointingly bland. He wrote over 120 quintets and nearly 100 quartets; apart from him the quartet's early history is largely Viennese, and even he had passed through Vienna at a formative stage before settling in Spain. In Vienna in Haydn's generation the quartet and symphony were cultivated by Karl von

Ordonez (1734–86), Carl Ditters von Dittersdorf (1739–99), and the prolific Bohemian Johann Baptist Vanhal (1739–1813). Ordonez was an innovator; certain works of the 1760s show unusual features such as thematic connections between movements (an idea more cultivated in the nineteenth century than the remainder of the eighteenth), and a high incidence of fugue. But by 1772 Haydn had composed at least twenty-two quartets; had he written no more, op. 9 and op. 17 would be counted among the best of the time. Even in this *galant* and popular context, Haydn's intellectuality appears in his subtly irregular phrasing and the growing intricacy of his polyphony. In op. 20 (1772; published 1774) the amplitude of the first movements brings his style closer to maturity than the fugal finales, and the minor-key quartets can be associated with the emotionally forceful *Sturm und Drang* symphonies. Aspects of these quartets, including the increase in formal counterpoint, were dutifully imitated by the young Mozart.

Haydn may have felt he could not surpass op. 20, or he may have been too busy with the Esterház opera, and with symphonies and baryton trios, to indulge in gratuitous composition. The Viennese quartet continued with Vanhal, whose expertly-written music never attains the egregious charm of Boccherini or the nervous high spirits of Haydn. In 1782 Haydn produced op. 33 and Vanhal turned to other genres. Less pusillanimous (or less discerning) composers continued to write quartets, such as the Bohemians Leopold Kozeluch (1747–1818), Franz Krommer (1759–1831) and Adalbert Gyrowetz (1763–1850), and the cosmopolitan Ignaz Pleyel (1757–1831). These men, however, are better remembered for other genres, in which no damaging comparisons can be made with greater masters. There is much to charm in the repertories for flute, oboe, clarinet or bassoon with a string trio or quartet (notably works for clarinet by Krommer, Hummel, the Finnish clarinettist Crusell (1775–1838) and Weber). Even if we repress the unworthy suspicion that this music is revived because greater composers neglected such groups, it remains true that singling out a wind instrument inevitably means a concertante rather than chamber ambience. Few followed the lead of Mozart in his elegant, idiomatic, yet discursive clarinet quintet. Krommer, however, is Mozart's most worthy successor in music for 'Harmonie'; his works for eight or nine wind players are lively and texturally inventive to a degree barely matched by Beethoven and Hummel.

In op. 33 Haydn claimed to have composed quartets 'in an entirely new and special manner'. Rosen argues that this is not mere salesmanship; he calls the integration of theme and accompaniment to the point of indistinguishability 'a revolution in style . . . the true invention of classical counterpoint'. Haydn achieved an athletic coordination and economy unique until Beethoven, a fact far more momentous than such novelties as calling the accelerated minuets 'Scherzo', or details like the opening of no. 1 (in D major, but the music proves to be in B minor), or the 'joke' ending of no. 2. The integration of themes between movements is barely concealed in no. 3 in C, whose first movement integrates the new counterpoint with the expansiveness of op. 20. Informed as they are by the spirit of *opera buffa*, the op. 33 quartets are also profoundly serious, and raise the medium to a new height – one scaled immediately, from another direction, by Mozart, but otherwise occupied until Beethoven's op. 18 only by a glorious succession of masterpieces from Haydn himself.

On the last day of 1782 Mozart began the quartet in G which he placed first in a set of six and published in 1785 as op. 10; Mozart dedicated 'the fruits of a long and laborious endeavour' to Haydn. The autographs show, for Mozart, an exceptional amount of cancellation and revision; this most fluent of composers found string quartets difficult, and his inhibitions, as well as his achievements, have coloured the medium ever since. By 1791, when Mozart died, Haydn had written eighteen more quartets, and Mozart only four. Most of 'op. 10' must rank with his greatest chamber music, but he appears more confident in other genres, including those he invented. The wonderful polychromatic quintet for piano and wind was imitated (by Beethoven, Danzi and Spohr), but never equalled. The wind works are the most loved in this restricted repertoire, and the trio for clarinet, viola and piano, known as *Kegelstatt* because of its alleged composition during a game of skittles, is among his most original conceptions, no doubt because it was written to be played with his friends.

Mozart's supreme chamber works are four string quintets, two from 1787 in C and G minor, and two from 1790–91, in D and E flat. His hopes of a lucrative subscription were not realized, and it was many years before the possibilities of this group were followed up, first in a Classicistic quintet by Beethoven (op. 29, 1801), then in an early masterpiece by Mendelssohn (op. 18, 1826). The contrast of

Mozart's C major and G minor quintets pre-echoes that of his last two symphonies, composed in 1788: one dark-hued, concentrated, passionate, the other luminous and expansive. To the usual four movements the G minor adds a slow aria before the finale, a daring and successful juxtaposition of pathos and geniality, and the D major has a slow introduction which recurs during the first movement, an exceptional event in Mozart. The E flat work is lighter than the others, but equally inventive in counterpoint, its last movement seemingly another high-spirited tribute to Haydn.

The apogee of Haydn's output, in all forms, is the set of quartets op. 76 published in 1799. There are several unusual features. Although as usual only one is in a minor key, three have minor-key finales. No. 2 in D minor has a nickname (*Fifths*) which alludes to a purely musical phenomenon, the main motive of the first movement. This, and the falling third in no. 3 in C, is developed with such concentration that the texture comes almost closer to fugue than sonata. No. 3 is the *Emperor*, its slow movement an undemonstrative act of patriotism, variations on Haydn's own imperial hymn. Almost every movement of the set contains some fresh feature, but no. 6 in E flat is the most capricious; it opens with a variation set followed by a fugue, its slow movement begins without a key signature and explores the harmonic universe before resolving in B major, the trio to the minuet consists of nothing but scales, and sonata form is withheld for the finale, which is based almost entirely on a motive of five notes. Op. 76 belies not only Haydn's age but the traditional image of 'Papa Haydn': rather we should see him as a prodigy of perennial youthfulness.

It has been suggested that Beethoven waited until Haydn had finished with a form before tackling it himself. Certainly this is true of the symphony and sonata, while his early trios are in the symphonic, rather than the piano sonata, mould. But Beethoven began writing quartets before the appearance of Haydn's op. 77, two superb works whose release for publication in 1802 signalled his inability to complete a full set (two middle movements exist for a third quartet, op. 103; they show that Haydn was still original at seventy). Beethoven had to work in the consciousness of both Haydn and Mozart, and also made a careful study of the excellently crafted quartets of his friend Emanuel Förster (1748–1823). Beethoven's op. 18 begins a series shorter, but more formidable to posterity, than Haydn's; and like Mozart's op. 10 it was the fruit of long travail, from

1798 to 1801. The order of publication is not that of composition. Beethoven chose to head the collection with an expansive work in F; its slow movement is particularly unlike those of his great predecessors in its morbid lyricism (Beethoven is alleged to have had the tomb scene of *Romeo and Juliet* in mind, and he was to refer to *The Tempest* in connection with the fiery D minor Piano Sonata op. 31 no. 2). Op. 18 no. 3, the first composed, is a polished tribute to Haydn, while no. 5 in A is demonstrably modelled on Mozart's quartet in A, к464. No. 6 in B flat includes a slow introduction to the finale, making a virtue of contrast, like Mozart in the G minor quintet, between a skittish allegro and a dour preface which Beethoven entitled 'Melancholy' (*La malinconia*). In places op. 18 has just a trace of prentice work, but the student is a genius whose power was to turn the quartet, and other genres, into new directions.

THE SYMPHONY

In the mid-eighteenth century, symphonies in three or four movements were equally common, with the three-movement form (conforming to the Italian sinfonia and the concerto) tending to predominate. The four-movement form results from the inclusion both of a true finale (usually in sonata form) and a dance movement (usually a minuet, later a scherzo). Circumstances might lead a composer to adjust a completed work: Mozart added a minuet to the three-movement no. 33, and deleted one of two from the *Haffner* (no. 35), turning an orchestral serenade into a symphony. In general, three movements were favoured in Italy, north Germany (including C. P. E. Bach) and France; and even in Vienna by Ordonez and Vanhal. It is a testimony to Haydn's influence that the four-movement form became normal before the end of the century. Mozart wrote his *Paris* symphony (no. 31) in three movements in accordance with local expectations. Eight years later Haydn's Paris symphonies (nos 82–87) all have four movements. The presence of two minuets, one on each side of a slow movement, in Austrian divertimenti and serenades may explain why the minuet or scherzo is sometimes placed second rather than third.

The changed implication of 'symphony' by 1830 may be summarized: fewer new compositions; larger orchestras; longer movements; wider contrasts in tempo. The slow movements become more singing, adagio predominating over the eighteenth-century andante ('walking speed') – with, however, characteristic exceptions in Beethoven. The fleet-footed, one-in-a-bar scherzo takes over from the pompous or bucolic minuet or *Ländler*; in Beethoven's First Symphony the title 'Minuet' is a joke, contradicted by the direction 'presto', and in his Eighth the minuet is an ornate anachronism. The distinction in genre is made clear in Beethoven's Septet op. 20 (1800), one of his most popular works which descends from the divertimento and includes both minuet and scherzo.

Although by no means universal, the slow introduction to the first movement became normal in late Haydn. It could be grandiose like the old French overture, or it might pose a harmonic problem as Mozart did in his C major Quartet (hence its common nickname, the *Dissonance*). In the finest examples the composer will contrive to be both majestic and mysterious, as in the short introduction to Haydn's last symphony (no. 104 in D). Longer examples by Mozart (nos 38 and 39) provided the model for four of Beethoven's symphonies. In most respects, however, and in most composers' hands, symphonic form continued on eighteenth-century lines, enlarged to suit new expressive needs but so ordered that audience expectations could be assumed by the composer and followed or, more imaginatively, played against.

No study of this size can hope to trace the history of the symphony without unwarrantable oversimplification, so many were the centres of production in the eighteenth century and so various their achievements. The *sine qua non* is a good orchestra; it did not have to be large. The disciplined forces of Mannheim, which Burney called 'an army of generals, equally fit to plan a battle, as to fight it', did not produce as imperishable a series of symphonies as Haydn, isolated in Hungary with more modest forces, nor could the magnificent orchestras of Paris boast as fine a repertory as Vienna. For Mozart the greatest orchestra seems to have been that of the Bohemian capital, for which he wrote his (anybody's) most difficult symphony to date (the *Prague*, no. 38) in 1786.

The 'Mannheim' type of symphony, contrasting brilliance with sentiment, was always close to the Italian type from which, indeed, it may have originated; it was exported to Paris, and the Italianate J. C. Bach, London's leading composer of symphonies, was strongly connected with Mannheim. The character of the symphony in

Germany was already serious, and C. P. E. Bach's late symphonies apply the style of sensibility to the larger canvas with considerable success. North German critics blamed the Viennese for frivolity, but it was they whose approach, an eclectic combination of *opera buffa* and learned styles, provided the foundation of the nineteenth-century symphony. Despite Michael Haydn, Pleyel and other Viennese symphonists already mentioned, the unquestioned leader of this school was Joseph Haydn, who was educated in Vienna and wrote his first symphonies there for Count Morzin.

Haydn's development is an extraordinary phenomenon, not least because, despite his isolation, it was followed so eagerly all over Austria, Germany and abroad. He blessed his employer even as he chafed at his loneliness: 'I could make experiments, observe what made an impression and what weakened it . . . . I could run risks. I was set apart from the world, with nobody to confuse me and intrude on my development; and so I was compelled to become original'. A less remarkable man might simply have relaxed. Haydn's restless spirit drove him, when nearly forty, to a development which placed the symphony on a new footing and laid the foundation for its later status as the highest form of musical art.

Not purely musical; several of Haydn's symphonies had picturesque or other extra-musical associations, such as the times-of-day symphonies (nos 6–8, *c.* 1761: *Le matin, Le midi* and *Le soir*) and no. 73, *La Chasse* (1781). In addition there are several works which employ liturgical melodies. Why, it is not easy to say; but these works, such as no. 22 (misnamed the *Philosopher*) and no. 49 in F minor (*La passione*), are far removed from the Rococo delights or ceremonial splendour normal in a symphony. A number evoke the church sonata by opening with a dignified slow movement. These, however, are in a minority, and Haydn never used a story, as Dittersdorf did, entertainingly and touchingly, in his symphonies after Ovid's *Metamorphoses* (*c.* 1785). Even Haydn's *Il distratto* (no. 60), with its absent-minded self-quotation and its violin-tuning joke, is not itself programmatic, but derives from incidental music to a comedy. Of the works which revolutionized the potential of the form, the best-known, because of their titles, are probably no. 44 in E minor (*Trauer*: Mourning) and no. 45 in F sharp minor (*Farewell*). No. 44 is a powerful, rather than mournful work, and *Farewell* applies only to the finale, Haydn's most serious musical joke: we see the musicians departing one by one, and the symphony ends with just two violins, but we hear an exquisitely graded diminuendo. Haydn was apparently hinting that the musicians were due for a holiday; to his credit, Nikolaus took the hint, rather than taking offence. Haydn was indeed fortunate in his employer.

These symphonies possess qualities which, if none is without precedent, combine to break the bounds of the *galant* style: urgent rhythm, with a marked increase in syncopation; stern energy in the principal motifs; succinctness of form – despite the introduction of a new melody in the centre of the first movement of no. 45, a lyrical interlude in the driving allegro; and an increase of severe counterpoint – no. 44 has a minuet in canon and no. 46 in B a sturdily contrapuntal development. The prevalence of minor keys is often remarked but should not be exaggerated; nos 46 and 47 (in G) are of similar calibre. 1772 is the *annus mirabilis* of the Classical symphony.

Haydn's greatest symphonies possess the energy and seriousness of the 1772 works tempered less by his occasional rough jokes than by the ever-present wit of a connoisseur. At the height of his career, in the Paris and London symphonies, the urge to powerful expression is undiminished but finds its place within a popular idiom, of Viennese origin, open, vivid, and appealing in its use of folk music (although this too can be enigmatic: why introduce a Croatian tune to a London

30 Concert room at Hanover Square, London, in which the impresario Salomon's concerts took place; Haydn's last twelve symphonies were first performed here.

audience, in no. 103?). Historians have noted the coincidence of the 1772 symphonies with literary *Sturm und Drang*. The musical origin of the driving, turbulent style comes, not surprisingly, from the theatre; the stupendous triumphing dance of demons in Gluck's *Don Juan* (1761) left to Haydn only the application to the symphony of a style developed for the theatrical grotesque. *Sturm und Drang* should only be used for music as an analogy, not to imply any causative literary origin; it signifies the stormy, stressful idiom which permanently enriched the symphonic language through Haydn's example. In 1773 Mozart, despite his Italian orientation, wrote a remarkable symphony in G minor with all the same characteristics; fifteen years later came his second G minor symphony, and the kinship to the first is obvious although the loose-limbed energy of youth has given way to the perfectly coordinated tensions of maturity. Mozart was not going through a phase of adolescent striving in either year, and in 1788 he worked simultaneously on three symphonies of totally different character. No. 39 in E flat is truly Olympian until its scintillating finale; no. 40 is the G minor; no. 41 is the apotheosis of the eighteenth-century C major symphony, courtly, grandiose, its expanses filled with ingenious counterpoint, above all in the fugal *tour de force* with which it ends.

Beethoven's First Symphony (1800) is his nearest approach to Haydn, but it shows a consciousness of Mozart as well as much originality of detail – not least the opening chord, a mild dissonance pointing to the wrong key. Its full scoring, in which early critics commented unfavourably on the predominance of the wind, may have derived less from Mozart than from orchestral music of Revolutionary France. Yet France produced only one important symphonist in this generation. Etienne-Nicolas Méhul (1763–1817) wrote five symphonies between 1800 and 1810, strongly under Haydn's influence but possessing a vigour and inventiveness which also appear in his operatic overtures.

In Vienna Beethoven began his own transformation of the symphony before Haydn's death, and his relatively small output acted as an inhibition upon his would-be successors. As early as no. 2 in D (1802) he enlarged the dimensions of the symphony to match his preference for full scoring. His model may have been Mozart's no. 38, in the same key. Both precede an exceptionally extended Allegro with an introduction of Baroque grandeur, the slow movements are both in 3/8 and use the woodwind with especial eloquence, and the finales are magnificent caprices; Beethoven merely added a Scherzo. No. 3 in E flat (1803), however, owes nothing directly to any model, and it marks an epoch in the history of the symphony and in Beethoven's compositional scale. In the exposition numerous ideas are already developed, but the development section subjects them to an unprecedented working-out as well as introducing a new melody (analysts have demonstrated its relationship to the main theme, but it still affects the listener as new). Beethoven changes the proportions of the movement; its development is considerably longer than the exposition, and the coda amounts to a fourth subdivision of almost equal weight. The noble funeral march is on a comparable scale; the mercurial Scherzo is correspondingly enlarged; the finale, developed from earlier works (the ballet *Prometheus* and the piano variations op. 35), breaks the bounds of variation form by incorporating developments, fugato, and a marvellous slow variation before the triumphant close.

The meaning of such a colossal work is not to be grasped from the often-told story of a dedication to Napoleon, withdrawn when he became Emperor, or by the almost tautological subtitle *Eroica*. The history behind this symphony is already complex; it is bound up with Beethoven's awareness of his growing deafness, expressed in the valedictory sentiments of the 'Heiligenstadt testament'. But neither biography nor revolutionary politics can account for the music itself. Despite the rigour of its forms it proclaims most strongly the freedom of the artist to work out his chosen material in accordance with the laws it generates. Boldness here repaid the composer; his critics have long been silenced.

CHAPTER EIGHT

Religious music in a secular age

The spirit of philosophical enquiry, both scientific and humanistic, inevitably associates itself with scepticism. Some of the most influential thinkers of the Enlightenment, notably Voltaire and Rousseau, were regarded as atheists. The discoveries of astronomy, overthrowing the idea that the sun (let alone the Earth) was the centre of the universe, made it inevitable that traditional beliefs should be questioned. Newton's passion for alchemy was forgotten, but his mathematical and physical discoveries were justly admired, and Blake depicts him in a fashion scarcely different from the godlike Urizen. Until the French Revolution, religious conformity prevailed, but the view of the world and of man upon which it was based was subtly undermined. The religious revival associated with Romanticism was powerless to stem the tide; the truths of Christianity were valued not because they were true but because they were beautiful.

We refer to one who shines in many fields as a 'Renaissance' man, but the type was well known in the eighteenth century. Goethe is an example of 'Enlightenment man', whose views on colour-perception are now of more interest to art historians than physiologists, but who was a more than amateur botanist in the age of Linnaeus and Buffon, and was statesman as well as poet, novelist and dramatist. It is a brave new world that has such people in it. Further discoveries of Pacific islands and in the Antipodes (Captin James Cook died in 1779) meant more noble savages whom the word of God could never have reached, and whom the cultivated European (and American) could patronize. Man's place in the natural order began to seem more complex, and more exciting, than his relation to his maker. 'Know then thyself, presume not God to scan; The proper study of Mankind is Man.' Pope did not imply, of course, that God should be forgotten, and Voltaire said that, if He did not exist, it would be necessary to invent Him. Pope anticipated the Encyclopaedist position: science and art are the product of human endeavour and their goal is the better understanding not of transcendental matters but of the world

116

31 *Newton* by William Blake (1795). A figure of Michelangelesque sublimity studies the mysteries of geometry.

and of ourselves, an attitude which accords well with the Neoclassical revival in its evocation of the Greek philosophical outlook. 'Go, wondrous creature! mount where Science guides, Go, measure earth, weigh air, and state the tides . . .' (Pope, *An Essay on Man*). Pope, himself a Catholic, was being ironic; his subject was the weakness of man. But others took such precepts literally.

In such an intellectual climate it is not surprising that for the first time the finest endeavours of European musicians were no longer dedicated to the church. The secular music of many composers since 1600 is of an importance at least equal to that of their sacred music; in Monteverdi, Purcell, Handel, or J. S. Bach sacred and secular are in some kind of balance. But the sacred music of the later eighteenth century and of most of the nineteenth is generally on a lower level of artistic achievement, even ambition, than secular composition. There are wonderful exceptions, notably Beethoven's Mass in D. But in general sacred music, to a far greater extent than the finest operatic and symphonic composition, became the product of conservatism, if not of routine. There is no sacred equivalent to the magnificent series of Haydn's quartets and symphonies, to the operas of Gluck and Mozart, to the instrumental music of Beethoven or the songs of Schubert.

The churches were themselves partly responsible for the fact that their liturgies were no longer the natural home of advanced musical art. Many traditions rejected instrumental music, or only allowed the organ; this prohibition was inimical to the sonata style. Politics also played a part: musical display, as an attribute of Catholicism, was inevitably suspect to Protestant nations. But the Catholic traditions were undermined from within, by reformers advocating austerity in worship and by Joseph II's restriction on the secular powers of the clergy, which meant a reduction in church patronage at the precise time (1783) when Austrian composers were at the forefront of developments in musical language.

Even where the participation of modern instrumental groups was permitted, there were no sacred musical styles to exploit the opportunity. Rather the secular (operatic) style was imported, to live uneasily beside a more austere tradition of contrapuntal writing. This tendency was already well advanced in the early eighteenth century, when J. S. Bach himself was affected by the prevailing taste for operatic music in church. But the naturally contrapuntal idiom of the greatest Baroque music remained compatible with the 'strict' style, even in solo vocal pieces. In the period of *style galant* a divergence of old and new styles became a gulf. The liturgical music of the Catholic tradition, including Pergolesi, Jommelli, Galuppi, and most of the sacred works of Mozart, alternates between an impersonal, admirably crafted fugal style and the expressive and decorative styles of opera, even *opera buffa*: the one an artificial, eighteenth-century view of the perfection of Palestrina's counterpoint as taught in the influential textbook of Johann Joseph Fux, *Gradus ad Parnassum*; the other natural, but inescapably secular in its associations.

The church remained, however, a major employer of the humbler sort of musician, the singers, organists and choirmasters who naturally continued to compose or adapt music (often from the best-loved operas) for the divine service. In Italy the orphanages and convent schools continued the outstanding musical traditions of Vivaldi's time, and in the mid-eighteenth century still employed major composers such as Galuppi, whose sacred output rivals in bulk

32 Engraving by J. E. Mansfeld from the *Gallery of Catholic Abuses*, showing a *prima donna*, a male singer, and part of the divided orchestra including military instruments (trumpets and drums).

his historically more significant contribution to opera. From 1740 to 1751 he was employed by the Ospedale dei Mendicanti in Venice, where his successor Bertoni, another successful opera composer, was still in office when the institution closed in 1777. From 1768, after his Russian period, Galuppi became chorus master at the Ospedale degli Incurabili (also in Venice). His duties had to be fitted around numerous trips abroad, whose object was the production of operas; yet from 1748 he was employed at St Mark's, where in 1762 he became *maestro di cappella*, the most prestigious musical appointment in the city. Even when abroad he supplied Venice with oratorios, mass settings, canticles and motets, and his last years were increasingly devoted to sacred composition. Venice thus continued the tradition we associate with Vivaldi, for all that he was literally forgotten; the Venetian 'Hospitals' (in effect Conservatories) preserved a fine instrumental tradition, and the *galant* style succeeded the Baroque in sacred composition. We may well regard this *galant* 'sacred' style as inherently unsuitable, but only if we also condemn the richly ornamented architecture of the churches, so similar to palaces, in which the performance took place.

Italian sacred music of the eighteenth century is very little explored today. The sheer vitality of the operatic tradition, whose style dominates so much solo music in masses and motets, is not the explanation, for the opera itself has scarcely been reappraised. The main reason for neglecting this vast corpus of sacred music is that historical tendencies – it is hardly a considered 'verdict of history' – have favoured German composers. If Mozart wrote the finest of all Italian *opere buffe*, we may well assume that the finest Italian oratorio is Haydn's *Il ritorno di Tobia* (1775, revised 1784). Yet this work stands alone in Haydn's output, whereas for an Italian it would be commonplace to write twenty or more oratorios.

Every Italian composer's training, and a considerable proportion of his output, was concerned with setting Latin texts for the liturgies. But the taste for opera was so pronounced that the ban on theatrical events in Lent was evaded by the oratorio, the music being to all intents and purposes the same. An early and much-loved example of the alternation of *galant* and strict styles was Pergolesi's *Stabat Mater*, and the medieval poem was also popular in settings by Jommelli and Haydn. Such music, blending nobility and ornament, influenced the great Austrian mass tradition, and in Italy it survived unscathed into the nineteenth century, to be cultivated by composers now known, if at all, for their operas: Pacini, Mercadante, Donizetti, Bellini, and of course Rossini, whose *Messa di Gloria*, written for Naples in 1820, is perhaps the summit of Italian composition for soloists, voices and

33 The Abbey Church of Ottobeuren in Bavaria, built 1748–66 by J. M. Fischer: late-Baroque extravagance, but a typical setting for *galant* Catholic church music.

34 The 'Salle de spectacle' used for opera at Versailles; designed *c.* 1748 but completed in the early 1770s, it was the last major addition to the château.

orchestra in this period. Italian styles are also to be heard in Mozart, especially the litanies and vesper psalms. Italian composers abroad contributed significantly to Catholic sacred music, for instance in the Mass and Requiem settings of Salieri and Cherubini.

A similar mixture of traditional forms and modern music appeared in music of the Russian Orthodox Church, and this continued even beyond a ban on 'concertos' (i.e. modern vocal compositions) imposed by Tsar Paul in 1797. His predecessor Catherine the Great (reigned 1762–96) invited Italians to St Petersburg and sent Russians to Italy. Among the former the ubiquitous Galuppi made use of traditional sacred melodies in his Italianate counterpoint, and the aim of a modern Orthodox style was furthered by Russians, notably Dmitry Bortnyansky (1751–1825), who made less use of traditional melodies. However, the stylistic isolation of the Orthodox Church, in keeping with its resistance to all liturgical change, was complete if only because it continued to exclude all forms of instrumental music.

Just as scepticism was more widespread in France, so were her sacred musical traditions less powerful; yet her conservatism in opera was matched by that in the church. Paris secularized sacred music, not by modernizing its style, but by transferring it to the concert room and treating it as an aesthetic object. The 'Concert spirituel' was a series usually given by musicians from the opera on church festivals, when the theatres were closed. In their early years the high point of these concerts was a grand religious work, by the Baroque master

Lalande or his popular successor Mondonville. Such works, being in Latin, could be readily imported when German music became fashionable; Haydn's *Stabat* was almost as popular as his symphonies, and in 1778 Mozart wrote additional movements for a *Miserere* by Holzbauer. Thus the French Grand Motet was replaced by Italianate Catholic music, but in a secular context of symphonies, concertos and operatic excerpts.

Although French cathedrals maintained their choral services, based on the choirschools (*maîtrises*) in which many musicians were trained, French sacred music was in decline before the Revolution, and the best composers contributed comparatively little. In 1786 Jean-François Lesueur (1760–1837) took over the direction of music at Notre-Dame de Paris. His attempt to introduce modern music into the Cathedral, justified in polemical writings, led to his dismissal the next year. The difference between his and Italian church music was that while the latter merely exploited the decorative qualities of the prevailing operatic idiom, Lesueur's intention was dramatic; and the authorities were not willing to perceive the Mass as theatre. Lesueur naturally turned his attention to opera, and his most massive work is on a biblical theme (*La mort d'Adam*, performed 1809), in a style indebted to his dramatic oratorios. He left an unusually large body of sacred music of all kinds, some composed when he was chapel master for Napoleon. Lesueur's exploratory style, in which conventional harmony is spiced with his own interpretation of ecclesiastical or Greek modes, and which exploits colour and variation of forces to a remarkable degree, was an example to the French nineteenth century, notably his pupils Berlioz and Gounod.

Where so much purportedly sacred music appears out of tune either with musical or intellectual currents, Classical church music attained a modern synthesis in Catholic Austria. The music is not necessarily more religious in feeling, certainly than its Protestant contemporaries; indeed, it is generally more compelling as an artefact than as the expression of transcendental insights. In particular, and with great significance for the future of choral music, it attached symphonic methods and intensity of development to a vigorous choral style which owes something to older models, especially the Italians and Handel.

Just as the symphony and string quartet were rooted in modest forms, so the Austrian symphonic mass originated in settings which aimed to get through the very long texts of the Ordinary (the Gloria and Credo) as expeditiously as possible. The *missa brevis* confined the orchestra to accompaniment and the briefest introductory flourishes. The Gloria and Credo begin with the second clause of the text ('Et in terra pax' and 'Patrem omnipotentem'), the first being given by the Cantor, and the texts were then composed in a single movement with at most a couple of changes of speed (usually for the central sections, 'Qui tollis' and 'Et incarnatus'). Clearly such forms are more practical for regular liturgical use than the multi-movement (or 'cantata') mass, which takes clauses of the text for elaborate, separate development, and could only be used on special occasions. The cantata mass reaches its apogee and its point of irreversible decline in Mozart's C minor Mass of 1782–3, written to celebrate his marriage. Had it been completed, this work would have been on a scale comparable to J. S. Bach's Mass in B minor. It shows no regard for liturgical unity; the impressive drama of 'Kyrie eleison' yields to operatic cantabile at 'Christe eleison', the 'Laudamus' is a vocal showpiece, 'Qui tollis' a weighty double chorus, 'Quoniam' a severely fugal trio. Appropriately enough, Mozart forged this extraordinary music into an Italian oratorio, *Davidde penitente*, in 1785.

The symphonic mass of the high Classical style represents a sensible compromise between the functional and aesthetic imperatives of the short mass and the cantata type. Making full use of the orchestra and a group of solo voices within choral movements allowed areas of contrast to be as pronounced as in the cantata mass while maintaining continuity. The whole Gloria and Credo (now including the first text clause) can be treated concisely without recourse to the *missa brevis* technique of singing different clauses of the text simultaneously. A three-part form can still be imposed on these texts: allegro for 'Gloria in excelsis', andante at 'Qui tollis', allegro again for 'Quoniam', possibly with something like a recapitulation, and with fugal elements in the last clause ('Cum sancto spiritu'). The Credo falls into a similar pattern, the lively tempo naturally resuming at 'Et resurrexit'. The shorter texts of the Ordinary can all be set as one movement, and musical forms related to the symphony can be deployed, their length sustained by word repetitions.

The mass, like the four-movement symphony, acquired norms of musical structure which composers could exploit without fear of alienating either the church authorities or the congregation (audience). Formal ideas could be imposed or modifications made to the traditional sequence of moods, so long as their place in the larger framework was clear. The reprise of the melody of the Kyrie at 'Dona nobis' in Mozart's *Coronation* Mass (1779) has a purely aesthetic intention, imposing a large-scale musical form with no liturgical function; it might even be considered liturgically impertinent.

The symphonic mass will always be primarily associated with the Esterházy court through the last six masses of Joseph Haydn, but the strongest support for this pinnacle of achievement lay in Salzburg, not only in Mozart but in over thirty years' output by Michael Haydn (1737–1806). Many good judges considered Michael at least his brother's equal in this field, and his fame was no less widespread; he composed a mass for the Spanish court in 1786 and one for Vienna, with the Empress taking a solo, in 1801. His masses contain all the essential elements of the form: solos and ensembles, a full range of choral textures, resourceful handling of the orchestra, and, except in commissions for special festivals, conciseness. We owe the symphonic mass partly to the unpleasant Archbishop Colloredo of Salzburg, whose insistence that services should last no more than forty-five minutes stimulated Michael Haydn (and Mozart) to devise the formal procedures necessary for its development.

War, as well as the abandonment of liturgical trappings, compelled austerity in daily musical life, and elaborate mass settings were increasingly confined to special occasions. Joseph Haydn's last six masses were all composed for the name-day of Princess Maria Hermenegild Esterházy. Some modern critics argue that since Haydn composed no symphonies after the twelve for London, his symphonic genius found its outlet here. Certainly the orchestra is at the heart of the matter. Expression also led Haydn to make small formal adjustments or contradictions to the normal pattern. Although a minor key was itself unusual, he made the Kyrie of the D minor Mass (1798: known as *Missa in angustiis* or *Nelson* Mass) a sombre symphonic allegro without the slow introduction of the previous two Masses; reverting to the slow opening in the next two, he then made the whole Kyrie slow in the last (1802, *Harmoniemesse*). The *Nelson* Mass has a Gloria of classic precision, with recapitulation at 'Quoniam', but the Credo begins with a sturdy canon and in its later stages resorts to the ingenious device of singing the clauses of the text on a single note, round which the orchestra weaves a brilliant symphonic development. Following certain symphonic slow movements, Haydn defied convention by bringing in trumpets and drums in the normally lyrical Benedictus (*Nelson* Mass). This work has an original organ part, the woodwind parts being a contemporary transcription, but in the last three Masses, like the late oratorios, Haydn developed an elaboration of wind writing whose only precedents are in Mozart (hence the name of his last work, 'Harmonie' meaning 'wind band').

These works were inspiring models to Hummel, whose considerable output of sacred music dates from his employment as concert master to the Esterházy court (1804–11). The court also commissioned, but did not enjoy, Beethoven's Mass in C of 1807, a fine if slightly uncharacteristic work from his 'heroic' period which is overshadowed by the much later Mass in D. No other liturgical form ranks with the mass in importance, but among canticles Joseph Haydn's splendid Te Deum (1800), a work on the scale of a symphonic Gloria, deserves mention.

The *missa pro defunctis* or requiem has some text in common with the Ordinary, but a quite distinct and sombre character. One of Michael Haydn's was written in 1771 for the obsequies of the Prince-Archbishop of Salzburg, Sigismond Schrattenbach; it must have been known to Mozart, whose own setting matches the seriousness for which Michael Haydn was often preferred to his elder brother. Mozart's Requiem has a legendary aura which has tended to disguise the poverty of the completion by his pupil Süssmayr. Enough authentic Mozart, in his ripest style, shines through for the work to have become the obvious model for later settings, including two each by his seniors, Michael Haydn and Salieri. The appositeness of the texts of death and judgment for a dramatic composer was again demonstrated by Cherubini in his first Requiem in C minor (Paris, 1816). Cherubini's contrapuntal mastery derived from training in the same Italian school as Mozart, and this is synthesized with the mastery of modern orchestral and vocal idioms developed in his operas. He wrote several masses between 1773 and 1825. The later ones were for the ceremonies of the restored Bourbon monarchy, which was, perhaps, hardly worthy of this grandly intellectual offshoot of the high Classical tradition.

Sacred music came as naturally to Cherubini, whose work was admired by Beethoven and Brahms, as to Lesueur; but Weber, writing for the Catholic court of Saxony, and Schubert, writing for whomever he could interest, were emphatically secular composers. Weber's masses are unforcedly operatic in their solo writing and their dramatization of parts of the text. Schubert's smaller masses are of almost rustic simplicity, and he also set the mass and requiem in German. Outstanding in his attractive but often uncharacteristic sacred music are the two great masses in A flat (1819–22) and E flat (1828); if the counterpoint often sounds archaic, like parts of Mozart's Requiem, the rich instrumentation and adventurous harmony provide many memorable incidents, if not a newly considered framework. These works, and Beethoven's second mass (Mass in D or *Missa Solemnis*) irresistibly suggest not a composer fulfilling a vital liturgical function, but one working at a major musical form. Schubert omitted clauses which his conscience would not accept; Beethoven added an exclamatory 'O' when musical expression required. Beethoven, moreover, failed by years to finish the work in time for its intended occasion, the enthronement of Archduke Rudolph as Archbishop of Olmütz (Olomouc), as well as producing a work far too long and difficult for liturgical use.

The greatest weakness of sacred music in this period is the divorce between the natural bent of the major composers and the uses to which music could be put in church. Hence the mass, once the musical foundation of the liturgy, survived as a kind of oratorio, a musical form for composers to exploit. Masses and oratorios were written for choral festivals in Germany and England. Even if their venue was a church, such events were, and remain, secular in essence, social gatherings and celebrations of musical art. Mass settings entered the market, forming the staple product of Vincent Novello's publishing enterprise during the 1820s; he issued them in vocal scores so that performers could dispense with the orchestra, and fed a growing demand from choral societies both with masterpieces and with spurious works like 'Mozart's Twelfth Mass'. The existence of a British market for Catholic music (sometimes furnished with English words) demonstrates the growth of a general taste for choral music which found expression in such events as the Birmingham, Norwich and Three Choirs Festivals. The choral works of Cherubini, Mozart, and especially Haydn's *Creation* provided a crucial link between the Handelian tradition and the nineteenth-century oratorio repertory soon to be enriched by Spohr and Mendelssohn.

The movements towards austerity in worship in the Catholic and Orthodox Churches were paralleled in the Lutheran service, which was gradually stripped of ornament and hence of musical elaboration. The tradition of such composers as J. S. Bach and Telemann was steadily whittled away; and in the development of more severely functional music for devotion, the running was made by less well-established Christian sects. They were not always musically sophisticated, but their singing was the direct outcome of conditions of actual worship. Even under the control of the British crown, the future United States of America acquired a measure of musical independence, and if worship at the frontier of European civilization was more fervent than stylized, it showed considerable originality. In 1770 William Billings, 'native of Boston', published *The New England Psalm-Singer*, with new melodies, a fresh approach to polyphony, and novel forms.

In England itself, the hymnody of the Anglican Church as well as of nonconformist sects was stimulated by the Methodist movement. Viewed from abroad, the most distinctive native element on the British musical scene was the continuity of Anglican choral music; English fidelity to an old repertory was maintained by publications in new, sometimes discreetly revised, editions, notably Greene and Boyce, *Cathedral Music* (three volumes, 1760–73). But the most notable composer of new sacred music, Samuel Wesley (1766–1837), cheerfully disregarded mere usefulness, and although Catholic worship was forbidden he wrote elaborate Latin settings in a *galant* style, some on a very large scale (his cantata on the psalm *Confitebor tibi Domine* (1799) lasts over an hour). Wesley also contributed to the Anglican service, was probably the finest English organist of the time, and was a leading spirit in the introduction of J. S. Bach's music to Britain. Mozart's pupil Thomas Attwood (1765–1838) pursued a career divided between the sacred and secular, contributing to the most characteristic English forms, the Anglican service and the Coronation anthem. The revival of Anglican music in the nineteenth century rested on a continuing tradition; among its foremost composers were Attwood's godson Walmisley and Wesley's son Samuel Sebastian.

If formal Christian worship was musically at a low point in the early nineteenth century, the religious spirit found other outlets. Until Bonaparte's Concordat with the Pope (1801), the French

Revolution carried the banner of anticlericalism, even suppressing Christian worship. In reaction to this perversion of Enlightenment scepticism, a religious revival came to be associated with Romanticism; in France its manifesto was Chateaubriand's *Génie du Christianisme* (1802). Like the political restoration of monarchy, much of the revival of church music was conservative, even reactionary, and it did not kill the Enlightenment's interpretation of the religious spirit, which contributed just as strongly to the greatest artistic manifestations of the nineteenth century: its architecture, its poetry, its music drama, even, in the hands of sceptical composers like Berlioz and Verdi, its ostensibly Christian music.

The highest achievements of music that consciously reflect the religious attitudes of Enlightenment are the oratorios Haydn composed in the last phase of his activity. Both *The Creation* (*Die Schöpfung*, 1798) and *The Seasons* (*Die Jahreszeiten*, 1801) have a conventional religious message, but they also reflect a more secular philosophy which turns inward upon mankind. They are not the first musical works to do so. *The Magic Flute*, whatever the nature of Mozart's allegiance to Catholicism or Freemasonry, is a religious work in a general sense, for it concerns pilgrimage and the achievement open to those who aspire to wisdom and righteousness. The influence of pre-Christian religion and the hinted identification of evil with the late Catholic Empress suggest anticlericalism, and tend to strengthen the case for regarding the opera as a statement of belief. Mozart's use of Masonic symbolism is only a superficial manifestation of the position: the positive message is far stronger than Mozart's conventional, though doubtless sincere, professions that Death is mankind's only friend. *The Magic Flute* treats death only as a possible consequence of aspiring to a higher life. It makes many statements – on marriage, the futility of vengeance, the place of an ordinary man (Papageno) in an enlightened society – but its primary message concerns the desirability of order, the rule of reason, and the need for a society governed by consent, and within which no individual, not even Sarastro, is indispensable: powerful he may be, but control is handed over in due season to the next generation, an organic succession, not a revolution.

The Magic Flute is supported by a body of explicitly Masonic music, the best of it by Mozart. It belongs, moreover, to a select class of works (including the late Haydn oratorios and Beethoven's Ninth

Symphony) whose association with words and ideas does not only lend them significance, but also permits them to illuminate the social and other circumstances which contributed to giving them birth. They also suggest the possibility of a framework for hermeneutic study of works with no text, for which an obvious starting-point is the group of Haydn symphonies which refer to music originating outside themselves, religious, socially functional, or folkloric.

Haydn's late style is illuminated by the great oratorios in which his long experience of symphonic, operatic and sacred composition is combined with the relatively recent impact of Handel. Both works originated from contact with England, which if not a hotbed of enlightened thought was an acknowledged leader in matters mercantile, scientific and political. The texts were finalized by the egregious Baron van Swieten, the enthusiast for Handel and J. S. Bach who had already involved Mozart with earlier music; *The Creation* is rooted in Milton and the Bible, and *The Seasons* in James Thomson's long poem.

The Creation, which achieved immediate international acclaim, tends to overshadow *The Seasons*, but from a musical point of view this is hardly just. *The Seasons*, with its symphonic prelude, its operatic duets, its noble choruses (in the manner of symphonic Mass movements, with solos), is a match for *The Creation* in every respect but its poetic framework. Even the onomatopoeic music, which Haydn disgustedly called 'French', is done sensitively and without detracting from the flow of the lovely trio no. 18, with its cows, fish, cricket and frog. The sunrise is more glorious than that of *The Creation*, though not lovelier than the dawning of human consciousness in Eden; and the instrumentation is still richer. *The Seasons* suffers from over-extended hunting, drinking and spinning choruses needed to fill out Autumn and Winter; Spring and Summer are masterly throughout. The trouble is less the actual words than the unreal social context of the 'characters'. The idealized scene in which the only dangers, but all the blessings, flow from nature, and in which the only outside interference is a tale of a lord easily outwitted, represents a condition of rustic life which cannot be taken seriously. More sympathetically, *The Seasons* can be understood as an allegory, not of conflicts within or between human societies, but of Man's place in the Universe; but it must be admitted that in this respect its message is muted in comparison with *The Creation*.

Few dramatic works open as impressively as *The Creation*. The 'Representation of Chaos' is in reality a magnificent orchestral portrayal of slow and difficult creation; every promising musical continuation is evaded, or rendered ambiguous, by subtle shifts in harmonic perspective and by kaleidoscopic instrumentation. With the arrival of light, the first day, and the overthrow of the rebellious angels, the oratorio moves to a marvellously fresh and inventive catalogue of the days of creation. The third part is an Eden barely disturbed by intimations of the Fall. The place of Man in the cosmic order, as in Pope's *Essay on Man*, makes a stronger impact than the conventional religious trappings. From chaos, viewed as it were by telescope (in the age of Herschel, composer and astronomer, whom Haydn met in England), we progress to reason: chaos is understood in relation to the desirability of order. The least directly biblical part, the dialogue of Adam and Eve, conveys a version of the message of *The Magic Flute*; the climax is the arrival of the skilled and understanding beast, Man, comprising man and woman in married partnership (it would have gone too far, no doubt, to match *The Magic Flute* by seeing them as equals; Eve declares her willing dependence). Veneration of mankind and its achievements is naturally subversive, both to régimes of privilege and to deist religion; it must be disguised by allegory, even one drawn from Scripture.

The development of public concerts led to a striking increase in serious choral writing divorced from religion, in which respect the late eighteenth century anticipates the great choral era to come. Unusual works include Haydn's 'madrigal' *The Storm*; *Carmen Saeculare*, written by Philidor to words of Horace for performance in London in 1779; and the immense choral ode (*Begravingskantata*) by J. M. Kraus for the obsequies of Gustav III of Sweden. In France, the overthrow of established religion and the monarchy did not displace music from public life. The Revolution bore the torch of the Enlightenment, and many musicians were sympathetic to its aims. At the same time this revolution of individuals stimulated collectivism and, like the English revolution of the previous century, nationalism: this was, as has already been observed, the age of national anthems. With no church, secular institutions required celebration and attracted religious fervour; when this found expression in festivities musicians were needed, as in church festivals, to enhance atmosphere and provide a framework for worship by means of hymns.

The short-lived and palpably artificial French cult of the Supreme Being, and other festal occasions, often held out of doors, required music on a large scale. Although their grandiose simplicity of harmony and massive instrumentation more often than not yield only an empty pomposity, certain works produced in direct response to the needs of the young Republic sowed the seeds of a monumental style culminating in the 'architectural' works of Berlioz. The first anniversary of the fall of the Bastille (14 July 1790), when France was still a kingdom, was celebrated by Gossec's Te Deum with over one thousand performers. Gossec (1734–1829), never a great force in the theatre and past his prime as a symphonist, was the chief composer of revolutionary hymns to liberty, nature and reason (the new divinities); substantial works were also contributed by Méhul, Cherubini, Lesueur and Catel, for concert performance, communal rendering, domestic use, or the theatre. They appealed as much to patriotic as to republican sentiment, and included the funereal – as in Cherubini's commemoration of General Hoche's death in 1797 – as well as the triumphal. Musically, however, the most important consequences of the French Revolution were not in these topical lyrics and monumental frescoes, but in dramatic music whose influence extended well into the next century when most explicitly revolutionary music had died a natural death.

35 An artificial hill, on which musicians are strategically placed, erected on the 'Field of Reunion' in Paris for the Festival of the Supreme Being in 1790.

CHAPTER NINE

Revolution and Romanticism in opera

Despite the Revolution and the subsequent European war, there was no break in the continuity of operatic traditions outside France. Musical and production styles, subject-matter and its treatment, changed gradually, partly as a result of French developments but also under the impact of new ideas in literature and the visual arts. Even in France, the fall of the Bastille in 1789 was only one of a series of events well enough spaced out for cultural life to maintain continuity, and the era of instability ended as early as 1798 with Napoleon's *coup d'état*. The last opera by an Italian in the Piccinni tradition was Zingarelli's *Antigone* (1790). Cherubini began his French career with a *tragédie lyrique*, *Démophon* (1788). Although the 'Académie Royale de Musique' was considered a symbol of the *ancien régime* and was the scene of a demonstration two days before the fall of the Bastille, it continued to restage its Neoclassical repertory, including Gluck, and to produce works which now celebrated the achievements of liberty, or of Napoleon, as they once had those of Louis XIV.

Even in France most of the innovations of the 1790s had been anticipated before the Revolution. They include the elaboration of *opéra comique*, and realism, even with conventional subject-matter. In the mid-eighteenth century grandiose settings were peopled with larger-than-life beings whose vocal skills and physical stature were enhanced by huge and ornate costumes. Under the influence of comedy, but also of the wider movement towards realism in acting styles, simpler and less constricting costumes were used in Neoclassical French opera and later in *opera seria*. The realistic novel and theatre, cultivating the natural, preceded the 'Gothick' cultivation of the supernatural, and without naturalism the latter would lose impact. First archaeology led designers to research appropriate settings and costumes for subjects legendary, historically verifiable, or (in comedy) modern; then they were compelled to rediscover the beauties of untamed nature (ill. 6). 'Modern' subject-matter was derived from imaginatively conceived literature not

36 The German tenor Anton Raaff (1714–97) in his last great role, Mozart's
Idomeneo (1781). He wears the full, stylized plumage beloved of his generation.

37 The French soprano Mme Antoinette St Huberty (1756–1812) in her greatest
role, Piccinni's Dido (1783). The relatively simple garment and crown show a trend
towards a plausible idea of the antique.

subject to Classical disciplines: the poetry of Macpherson (the Ossian
forgeries), the novels of Scott, the plays of Schiller. Realism was an
attribute of *Sturm und Drang*, and of the developing interest in
folklore. These anticipations of Romanticism were well established
before the turn of the century and affected operas whose musical
idiom we would now tend to label Classical.

French revolutionary opera, however, was fired by the spirit of the
times to synthesize these tendencies and mark a definite break with
the formalities, of style and category, of the eighteenth century.
These operas seldom carry an explicitly political message. They are
realistic in that their usually happy endings are brought about by
humans rather than divine intervention: a friendly general or minister
confirms the victory of the good but weak over the evil but strong.

This scarcely reflects the reality of the often short-lived and morally equivocal revolutionary leadership. The more politically explicit the opera, the more black-and-white its ethics; there is more genuine moral conflict in Méhul's semi-serious romances than in the clash of freedom and tyranny of 'rescue' opera. But human ingenuity in overcoming tyranny is a notion sufficiently vague to provide a multitude of plots, which a new generation of librettists hastened to exploit.

Attempts to adapt Neoclassical tragedy to the *comique* genre produced a masterpiece, Cherubini's *Médée* (1797), but it was a failure with the public and its subsequent reputation derived from performances abroad. Successful operas were not necessarily topical, however. The bourgeois 'tearful comedy' was the favoured genre; Beaumarchais' sequel to *Figaro*, *La mère coupable* (1792), shows the Almavivas reduced to dependence on their servants and beset by a sponger, the 'new Tartuffe' of the subtitle. Grétry continued to compose without much success, but his natural heir in comedy, Nicolas-Marie Dalayrac (1753–1809), adapted better to changing taste. His reputation was founded on the 'tearful' *Nina, ou la folle par amour* (1786), in which love drives the heroine mad, then cures her; the libretto was adapted for Paisiello and Paer. The 'gothick' taste for prisons and monasteries is reflected in Dalayrac's *Camille* (1791) and *Léon* (1798), derived from Anne Radcliffe's *Mysteries of Udolpho*. H. M. Berton (1767–1844), in *Les rigueurs du cloître* (1790), combines a nunnery with anticlerical sentiment and a rescue.

High comedy and romance, without social and political implications, were just as acceptable, and the career of France's most original composer of this generation was founded on them. Méhul achieved a remarkable success with *Euphrosine* (1791). It is subtitled 'the tyrant corrected', but its plot concerns love and jealousy in an intimate circle: it is no tract for the times. It was admired for its charm, but still more for its dramatic commitment; the duet 'Gardez-vous de la jalousie' became Méhul's most celebrated movement. Both *Euphrosine* and *Mélidore et Phrosine* (1794) make use of recurring motifs. This device, hinted at by Méhul's mentor Gluck, was used extensively in Lemoyne's *Electre* (1782), but it was from Méhul that it passed to Weber and thence into the main stream of Romantic opera, eventually to become the symphonic leitmotif. *Mélidore* and *Ariodant* (1799) are love stories in which, with the Ossianic *Uthal* (1806),

Méhul fully exploits another novelty of French Revolutionary opera, the expressive use of colour. Veiled chords on stopped horns, penetrating low woodwind, strange string sonorities (*Uthal* has no violins) are legitimate effects in a music free of stylization in which colour becomes substance. Méhul flouts other conventions for the sake of the drama, bringing a voice into an overture (*Uthal*) and ending music on a dissonance, to plunge into spoken dialogue (*Mélidore*). If these works have topical significance, it is only by analogy between political and natural upheavals. 'Rescue' need not be from any human agent but from a stormy sea and rocky coastline, as in *Mélidore* and Kreutzer's *Paul et Virginie* (1791), based on the popular novel by Bernardin de Saint-Pierre. These works also deal with individual dilemmas occasioned by social, rather than political, tensions; they are the true prototype of Romantic opera.

The Florentine Luigi Cherubini (1760–1842) settled in France in 1786 after gaining experience in Italian opera. Like his compatriot Lully he became a leading figure in French musical life for half a century; he was among the founders of the Paris Conservatoire and its Director from 1822. His musical style is closer than that of his French colleagues to the Viennese, and his greatest artistic triumph was his visit to Vienna in 1805. The heroic comedy *Lodoïska* (1791) is an archetypal rescue opera. Its reflection of modern politics is, however, minimal; it is mainly an exciting story, and except for a cowardly descendant of Leporello the characters belong to the traditional ruling classes. The tyrant is the incarnation of evil, the good are unflawed, the genre being a new stylization, a heightened naturalism: it could happen, although it surely would not. The local (Polish) colour, the Tartar chieftain who comes to the rescue, the spectacular climax, are matched by music of vigour and resourcefulness, although Cherubini is always prone to develop situations at excessive length. Another *Lodoïska* by Rodolphe Kreutzer (1766–1831) was produced within two weeks of Cherubini's, and was rather more popular at first.

'Rescue' as an operatic dénouement was not a new idea; Grétry's *Richard Coeur-de-Lion*, although banned as royalist, was an obvious precedent. With Cherubini's later masterpiece *Les deux journées* (also known as *The Water Carrier*: 1800) those rescued are still aristocrats, but the humble characters take the risks on their behalf. The moral is indeed 'liberté, égalité, fraternité'. National liberation is evoked in Grétry's *Guillaume Tell* (1791), whose Swiss local colour was excelled by Cherubini in *Eliza* (1794). *La caverne* (based on Lesage's *Gil Blas*) is a tale of Romantic banditry, and was Lesueur's first opera (1793: Méhul's *La caverne* came two years later).

The *locus classicus* of this Romantic-realist genre is a rescue opera which claimed to be true, a 'fait historique'. *Léonore, ou l'amour conjugal*, text by Bouilly, was set by Pierre Gaveaux (1760–1825) in 1798. A wife disguises herself as a youth, traces her husband to where he is unjustly imprisoned by a personal enemy, and saves him with the help of a sympathetic plebeian, the jailor, and a timely visit from the King's minister. Gaveaux was an all-round musician; as a tenor, he sang Florisky in *Lodoïska* and Florestan in his own *Léonore*. It is worth recalling that roles in these operas require musicianship, acting ability and stamina, rather than a virtuoso's technique. Gaveaux also published and sold music. His opera would have remained merely typical had it not aroused the interest of more gifted composers, for the libretto soon joined those on the international circuit. French libretti were a valuable resource for Germany so long as the music had not succeeded there, and for Italy which had no use for French music anyway.

Simon Mayr (1763–1845), a German who spent most of his career in Italy, set a translation of Bouilly's *Les deux journées* for Milan as early as 1801. The librettist Rossi translated and adapted *Ariodante* and *Eliza*, previously set by Méhul and Cherubini, and *Léonore* as *L'amor conjugale* (designated *dramma giocoso*) in 1805; all were set by Mayr. Ferdinando Paer (1771–1839), who later worked in Paris under Napoleon's patronage, wrote a *Lodoïska* in 1804 for Bologna, and *Leonora* in Italian for Dresden the same year. The attraction of these subjects was their novel blend of the serious and light-hearted; they established a new mode between the traditional extremes, the *dramma semiseria*, as Paer's *Leonora* was termed.

Mayr and Paer were among the most important precursors of Rossini and nineteenth-century Italian opera in general. The French vogue reached Austria with the successful production of Méhul and Cherubini operas by German companies; two versions of *The Water Carrier* were given in Vienna on consecutive nights in 1802. Beethoven, who had long been in search of a libretto, settled upon *Léonore* at about the same time as Mayr and Paer. But whereas they saw in it an opportune subject, touching and contemporary, Beethoven seized upon its ethical content. By modelling himself on

Cherubini he emphasized the serious aspect of the story, reducing the comedy in which it was originally framed to insignificance. (Beethoven criticized Mozart's lavishing of fine music on immoral subjects; he may have felt that the love of the jailor's daughter for the disguised Leonora was hardly in the best of taste.)

When he wrote *Leonore* (1804–5) Beethoven had some dramatic experience, besides having played viola in numerous operas in Bonn. He had composed two ballets, some incidental music, and the oratorio *Christus am Oelberge* (1803–4), which contains fine music but suggests some discomfort with the operatic aspect of the genre (as does Schubert's fascinating fragment of 1820, *Lazarus*). There are signs of uncertainty in the first version of Beethoven's only opera, given in November 1805 at the Theater an der Wien. It is over-extended (in three acts), and was preceded by the massive overture *Leonora no. 2*, which upstages the first-act comedy. Nevertheless it is a remarkable achievement. Strong meat for the Viennese, as Joseph II said of *Don Giovanni*, it might have fared better had not military reverses filled the Austrian capital with French troops. A modest revision, with the overture *Leonora no. 3* and running the first two acts together, did no better the next year.

We owe it to Beethoven's acute self-criticism, as well as to his prestige, that a substantially revised version appeared at the Kärntnerthor Theater as late as 1814, the libretto having been thoroughly overhauled by the manager, Treitschke. Several numbers were omitted, the first of the two acts received a new finale, the opening numbers were reordered (one consequence being a fourth overture). There were numerous revisions and retouchings, and the title *Fidelio* was finally adopted.

There are arguments for preferring the original version: its sub-plot is given time to work out, its dénouement is more fraught with peril (the scene remains the prison to the end, and the couple's rapturous duet is sung with their fate still in balance). But several numbers cannot survive knowledge of the revision, particularly Florestan's scene which opens Act II. The revised dénouement owes more to Leonora's efforts than to the jailor and minister, and in a new finale, the scene changes to the courtyard, the prisoners find the light, and with the villain banished Leonora herself loosens her husband's chains. The 1805–6 *Leonore*, like the *Prometheus* ballet and *Christus am Oelberge*, is a work which requires some apology. *Fidelio* is a masterpiece and belongs with the symphonies, *Egmont*, and the Mass in D among Beethoven's greatest large-scale works. It is not the foundation of nineteenth-century German opera, however; rather it is a culmination of opera's response to the Enlightenment and revolution, appropriately revised in the year of Napoleon's exile in Elba, in time for the Congress of Vienna. And in the chorus of prisoners in the first finale, the heroic aria of Leonora, Florestan's patient suffering, above all in the final hymn of love and freedom, Beethoven elevates opera to the sublimest religious plane.

French armies conquered Italy; the politics of revolution and reaction affected everyone, no less than in France and more than in most northern countries where régimes were less liable to sudden upset. Yet Italian opera of the early nineteenth century exhibits a more marked continuity than that of any other nation. Such change as there was appears in the stories used rather than in methods of adapting them or the musical fashions in which they were clothed. No doubt this continuity is partly the result of an unshaken confidence that opera and Italian opera were virtually synonymous. Italian musicians continued to be in demand everywhere; Italian opera companies remained obstacles to national opera in England, Russia and Germany; Spontini and Rossini were dominant forces in France.

38 Leonora rescues Florestan; illustration by V. R. Grüner (1815) of the dungeon scene from Beethoven's *Fidelio*; as Pizarro draws she steps between the men exclaiming 'First kill his wife!'

39 The immense auditorium of the San Carlo theatre, Naples (cf ill. 11), showing seating in boxes and parterre only, the painted ceiling, and the crowded stage.

The senior generation of Italian composers at the turn of the century was highly respected; Cimarosa and Paisiello, not Gluck and Mozart, were the classics of the repertory. Among the most popular operas of the period was Zingarelli's *Romeo and Juliet* (Milan, 1796), which kept the stage for thirty years. Zingarelli (1752–1837) was of generally conservative outlook, and he taught both Mercadante and Bellini in Naples. Mayr, who taught Donizetti in Bergamo, and Paer were open to French influence in choice of libretti rather than musical style, at least until Mayr's Neoclassical *Medea in Corinto* (1813). Their music does not reflect the nascent Romanticism of its subject-matter, being post-Mozartean in style, or like Cherubini without his austerity and vigour. The generation of the 1790s – which in addition to Rossini includes Saverio Mercadante (1795–1870), Giovanni Pacini (1796–1867), and Gaetano Donizetti (1797–1848) – was brought up to continue a tradition which none of them seriously questioned. The considerable changes wrought by about 1840, the beginning of Verdi's career, came about by evolution, not revolution.

The well-established division between serious opera and comedy remained fundamental, both types continuing an unbroken tradition; Rossini used the Paisiello libretto for *Il barbiere*, and Mercadante set two Metastasio libretti for Turin in the 1820s. Extreme genres were *azione tragica* and *farsa*; between them, and

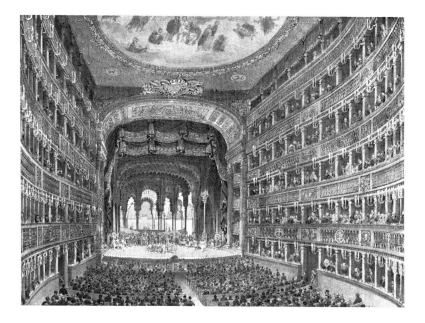

becoming recognizably a more modern type of opera, lay the *dramma* (or *melodramma*) *giocoso*, the *farsa sentimentale*, and other designations which may be loosely termed *opera semiseria* (examples are Rossini's *The Thieving Magpie* (*La gazza ladra*: Milan, 1817) and Donizetti's *Emilia di Liverpool* (Naples, 1824)). The blending of comedy, sentiment and seriousness relates closely to the modern French libretto, but most librettists preserved the verse-forms and high-flown expressions typical of the eighteenth century even when their subjects were new. The intermediate genre reflects new literary sources. Various operas murdered Shakespeare – after Zingarelli's came Vaccai's (1825) and Bellini's (1830) settings of *Romeo and Juliet*, preceded by Rossini's *Otello* (1816) and Mercadante's *Amleto* (1822) – or treated Scott in cavalier fashion, Rossini leading with *La donna del lago* (1819). Donizetti's *Elisabetta* (1829) is significantly based on a French 'Scott' libretto, Scribe's *Leicester* (set by Auber, 1823).

Variety of subject and designation, however, does not mean that the essentials of Italian opera were undermined. Much changed; the chorus is used more, the orchestration is more elaborate (Paer was influenced by Mozart, and Mayr was after all a German). The ideal form still remained the serious opera dominated by singers; and as in the eighteenth century the principal musical form remained the aria. It remained so throughout most of the nineteenth century as well.

It is tempting to see Gioachino Rossini (1792–1868) as a revolutionary, so flamboyant does he appear among his estimable but mediocre predecessors. In fact he was more like Napoleon, a stabilizing influence: conqueror of the Italian South, then of other nations, but also a codifier of laws. The 'Code Rossini' contained novel elements but it was a rationalization more than a reform, intended to control but also to placate those with influence (singers and managers). Rossini fixed the large formal strategies of serious opera, the conventions which were both to assist and to plague Verdi, and worked them out also, on a smaller scale, in comedy: the multisectional duet, the rondo finale ('Nacqui all'affano' in *La cenerentola*), the double aria. The latter begins with a slow movement; information or an event permit a change of mood, and the second movement, the 'cabaletta', is usually brilliant in style (an example from Rossini's first successful serious opera, *Tancredi* (Venice, 1813), is 'Tu che accendi', with the cabaletta 'Di tanti palpiti', one of the great show-stoppers of the century).

As in the eighteenth century, serious opera favoured high voices, and when the castrati departed women often took the lover's role (including Romeo in Bellini's opera); high voices, traditionally associated with heroic characteristics through their virtual monopoly of *opera seria*, are also generally more suited to coloratura. Rossini is credited with bringing vocal ornamentation under control by writing out what might have been improvised (this was a gradual process, not simply the result, as is often stated, of his move to Naples in 1815, the year of *Elisabetta, regina d'Inghilterra*). But unlike Gluck Rossini did not use compositional control to reduce ornamentation: he took advantage of the skills of the Naples singers to make unornamented performance impossible (it was doubtless rare in any case), and delighted his performers by outstripping them in baroque inventiveness. Arias were still tailor-made for singers, yet in revivals, with the composer away, they would often insert a favourite piece, one of their 'suitcase arias' (*pezze di baule*). Rossini himself (this time like Gluck) frequently reused arias in later works, wrote new passages on old motifs and transferred overtures; the one made famous as *The Barber of Seville* was serving for the third time.

Within his own conventions, Rossini was able to develop as a dramatist partly by modification of set forms. The overture was gradually abandoned, or elements from it reappear in the opera (*La*

40 A scene from Rossini's *Semiramide* designed by A. Sanquirico for Milan (1824); a serious attempt is made to recreate the style of ancient Nineveh.

cenerentola, Semiramide). Regimented blocks of solo virtuosity are broken up by an actively participating chorus; greater continuity, and massing of forces, reflects French influence, including that of Spontini. With *Mosè* (1818) and *Maometto II* (1820), Neapolitan operas he was to adapt for Paris, Rossini's move to France begins to seem inevitable. His serious operas in Italian are concluded with *Semiramide* (Venice, 1823), an icy, jewel-encrusted monster of a tragedy on a subject drawn from Voltaire and used by Gluck.

Less formal elements directed towards dramatic truth in serious operas included local colour and an almost folk-like simplicity of melody for a few well-chosen numbers. Amid the bustle of Rossini's earlier style, the gratuitous but tenderly evocative gondolier's song and Desdemona's 'Willow song' partially redeem *Otello* to a posterity which knows Verdi, while the compellingly simple prayer from *Mosè* is a foretaste of the great choral Romantic operas. Rossini's serious works are historically his most important; even the most original of his successors, Donizetti, Bellini, Verdi himself, naturally emulated him. But he himself said he was born for comic opera. It is true that his best comedies hardly affect the development of the genre; Donizetti would have approached comedy as he did even without Rossini's example. But the exuberant spirits of a manic-depressive burst irresistibly forth in the ensembles, crescendos, and patter-arias of Rossini's comedy. Despite his slowness of harmonic movement (which makes a Rossini presto equivalent to a Mozart andante) the bright primary colours of the orchestra and the impertinently memorable tunes brought Rossini a success equal to, more deserved, and more lasting, than that of his tragedies.

The subject-matter of Rossini's and Donizetti's comedy is familiar: faked magic (Donizetti, *L'elisir d'amore*, 1832); fairytale (Rossini, *La cenerentola* (*Cinderella*), 1817); the buffoon outwitted by young love (*The Barber of Seville*, 1816); Europeans in Muslim lands (*L'italiana in Algeri*, 1813), and in a reversal of the usual location of this conflict of the homely and the exotic, *Il turco in Italia* (1814). Exotic subjects were popular everywhere (e.g. Boieldieu, *Le calife de Bagdad*, 1800; Weber, *Abu Hassan*, 1811). Rossini's most successful semi-serious opera, *La gazza ladra,* might be termed a 'reprieve', rather than rescue, opera, like Monsigny's *Le déserteur*.

The international phenomenon of Rossini-mania can only be understood if we recall the immense attraction of all things Italian to the northern part of Europe. If anything the wars enhanced it; Italy absorbed Byron and Stendhal for many of their most creative years (*La chartreuse de Parme* is a wonderful 'semi-serious' novel treating of romance and politics in post-Napoleonic Italy). Writers, painters and musicians were sent to Rome by the Paris Institute to sharpen their perceptions; Germans, like Meyerbeer, still turned to Italy when they saw no great future for their art at home. Rossini-mania is brilliantly evoked by Stendhal in his otherwise unreliable *Life of Rossini* (1824), written at its height when the hero was only thirty-two. The disease was infectious; Beethoven complained of it in Vienna; Schubert succumbed, but in doing so fertilized his mature style and preserved his independence of Beethoven. Among Rossini's Italian successors the most distinctive new voice to be heard in the late 1820s was that of Vincenzo Bellini (1801–35), whose musical strength was a very personal, ornate and widely-arched melody which at its best is as sensitive a conveyor of dramatic meaning as Germanic harmony or motivic transformation. Bellini's finest works are a unique Italian contribution to Romanticism, and his early death left a gap which, despite the generation of the 1790s, only Verdi could fill.

Until late in the nineteenth century, London continued to equate opera with Italy, and French or German operas were as likely to be sung in Italian as English. Opera could still be 'exotic and irrational' in the native language; the near-masterpiece of its genre, Weber's *Oberon* (1826), is not far from Purcellian semi-opera in form. But Paris, while it increasingly enjoyed Italian opera in the original, was still able to assimilate Italianate composers to indigenous traditions, thanks to the esteem and financial resources enjoyed by government-backed opera houses. When the force of the Revolutionary decade was spent, Napoleon's Empire developed its own style of austere ornamentation upon a self-consciously Neoclassical foundation. Napoleon as liberator remained a powerful Romantic image, but as Emperor he became virtually indistinguishable from the dynastic monarchies of Europe into which he married in 1810. Legendary heroes, notably Ossian, the feminine figure of liberty, the virtues of ancient Rome, music, decoration and literature were used for an image-promotion whose assiduity rivalled that of Louis XIV. On the whole Beethoven was right to feel disgust.

Napoleon's own musical taste was for traditional Italian fare, but

41 A. L. Girodet, *Homage to Napoleon* (1802); Ossian receives the generals of the Republic into Valhalla.

prestige demanded the revival of the Opéra, and the Emperor supported the belated production of Lesueur's best work, *Ossian*, in 1804. This expansive drama matches the Romantic extravagance of Macpherson's forged epic poetry, to which Napoleon was also partial, and in whose authenticity, despite the evidence, Lesueur firmly believed. Bardic harps feature in the evocative instrumentation, and Lesueur used inflections alien to the major–minor system to give his music a Celtic flavour. The subjects open to operatic exploitation now included Bible stories, formerly forbidden the stage. In *Joseph*, an *opéra comique* (1807), Méhul explores the moral dilemmas of Joseph and Simeon with his usual penetration, and he developed an austere, Neoclassical colouring which did not prevent this being his greatest international success. Kreutzer's *Abel* was given at Malmaison the same year and at the Opéra in 1810, following Lesueur's immense *La mort d'Adam*.

The master of Empire opera, however, was an Italian, Gaspare Spontini (1774–1851). Spontini's early Italian career was relatively undistinguished, but in France he was favoured by Napoleon's first Empress, Josephine, to whom he dedicated a curious *opéra comique*, *Milton* (1804). His masterpiece, *La vestale*, a Neoclassical lyric tragedy, was given at the Opéra in 1807; *Fernand Cortez*, more obviously in tune with Imperial foreign policy, was performed before Napoleon in 1809. Despite its popular story-line, its sumptuous setting, its wealth of Spanish and exotic colour, and Spontini's temperate but forceful lyricism, *Cortez* was less successful, at least until its thorough revision in 1817. But while *La vestale* is unquestionably one of the finest operas of the period, it is a retrospective rather than revolutionary triumph, and its powerful lyricism and resplendent orchestration decorate a dramatic image well known in earlier operas such as Gluck's *L'innocenza giustificata*. The happy ending is ensured in pre-revolutionary style by divine grace; as in Gluck's *Iphigénie* operas, armed intervention on behalf of the hapless victim (Julia, the erring Vestal), is not enough.

The second act of *La Vestale* is Spontini's supreme achievement, built in a single span analogous to a crescendo. Julia is formally admonished and left to guard the sacred flame. She meditates on the conflict between love and her vow of chastity in a two-part aria of deep lyrical exploration and frenzied abandon. Her lover arrives; their duet leads to catastrophe. The sacred flame is extinguished, and in a massive choral finale Julia refuses to reveal her lover's identity and is condemned to be buried alive. The nobility of style, backed by rich orchestration, and the masterly control of dramatic rhythm, make *La vestale*, as Wagner and Berlioz acknowledged, both a worthy successor to Gluck and ancestor to their own works.

Ever-widening gaps separated Spontini's later operas – not the only respect in which he anticipated Meyerbeer – and most were produced in Berlin, where he was general director of music to the court from 1820. Despite his influence on Wagner, he acted as a conservative, anti-Romantic force in German opera, appearing particularly hostile to Weber at the time of *Der Freischütz*, and his legacy is the development of French grand opera, for which *Cortez* is the true prototype.

Opéra comique continued to flourish under the Empire and Restoration. The late works of Dalayrac and Méhul belong to the Empire, as does much of the successful career of Adrien Boieldieu (1775–1834). Boieldieu was an elegant melodist whose charm won him friends everywhere. He divided his attention between continuing the serious *opéra comique* of the Revolutionary decade (*Beniowski*, 1800) and the most cheerful of comedies; *Jean de Paris* (1812) easily won him back the Paris public after eight years' absence in Russia. In 1825, at the height of Rossini-mania, Boieldieu won an international triumph with a semi-serious opera loosely based on Scott. *La dame blanche* did much to maintain the independence of French style, but it belongs to a tradition already established within *opéra comique* in which the Romantic atmosphere is tempered by a musical language of easy charm and carefully moderated brilliance which would repel nobody and delight the generally unadventurous public.

Boieldieu's triumph was preceded by the *Leicester* of Daniel-François-Esprit Auber (1782–1871). Auber's operatic career lasted over sixty years to 1869, but his best work predates 1835, and cultivates the lighter end of the *opéra comique* spectrum (with a fondness for comic bandits: *Fra diavolo*, 1830). The librettist for nearly all his works, and for *La dame blanche*, was the deplorably fertile Eugène Scribe (1791–1861). Scribe ranged from the frothiest comedies through the semi-serious to grand opera, where his first triumph was Auber's *La muette de Portici* (1828). This touching story of a mute, who mimes to remarkably articulate orchestral music, is grafted onto the increasingly popular type of plot which deals with political insurrection. A performance at Brussels in 1830 ignited the revolt which led to the independence of Belgium. Auber's surprisingly powerful orchestration and dynamic rhythms were never again matched by him, and he may have been conscious of his debt to a far greater composer already resident in Paris.

Rossini came to France in 1824 to direct the Italian theatre, and was quickly involved in plans to write French operas. *Le siège de Corinthe* (1826) is yet another claimant for consideration as the 'first' French grand opera. Rossini may have been moved to adapt *Maometto II* by the Greek War of Independence; Byron had died at Missolonghi in

1824. Rossini thus allied himself to the growing cause of Romanticism, without prejudicing his musical hold over a wider public. In 1827 he added a French version of *Mosè*. In these adaptations Rossini simplified the ornaments, for which French singers were not trained; melodic directness compensates for some reduction in scale when musical forms are compressed into a more continuous structure. In short, like Piccinni and Spontini before him, Rossini accommodated himself to the patterns of French opera. He also introduced a fuller, indeed noisier, orchestration, which coupled with remarkably lavish standards of *mise-en-scène* made French grand opera the brash, larger-than-life affair it remained during the extended reign of Meyerbeer.

In 1826 Berlioz wrote an unperformed opera, *Les francs-juges*, and Victor Hugo (1802–85) published a manifesto, the preface to *Cromwell*, in which he rejected Classical ideas of beauty, with their restraint and strict forms, declaring that the grotesque and disordered were also beautiful. In 1827 Rossini produced *Le comte Ory*, his one collaboration with Scribe and his most delightfully risqué comedy, and Shakespeare was suddenly the rage in Paris. Rossini's last stage work, based on Schiller, was *William Tell* (1829). His only new work for the Opéra, *Tell* capitalized on the success of *La muette* as well as of *Le siège* and *Moïse*. Common themes are the struggle for liberation, and national conflict engendering conflicts of loyalty; in *Tell*, heroism is pitted against both human and natural forces. This huge canvas of history and legend, enriched with local colour, inspired the composer's most broadly conceived and dramatically compelling music.

Yet Rossini's personal involvement in artistic movements and politics was slight. Nationalism and political liberty were in the air, and the magnificent reunion of rebel cantons at the climax of Act II of *Tell* carries a threat, or promise, which Rossini himself did not fulfil. In 1830 Charles X fled from the July Revolution, ending the Bourbon monarchy; Hugo's *Hernani* finally breached the Bastille of Neoclassicism in French spoken theatre; and Berlioz's *Symphonie fantastique* was completed. The Napoleon of opera retired from the fray, leaving the field clear for Meyerbeer. *Tell*, the summation of his achievement, stands uncomfortably at a crossroads between older and newer musical languages. The French were already aware of a subtler harmonic and instrumental palette, fresher and more concise musical forms, an apparently more authentic folk music: with the knowledge of Weber, France began to return the compliment of influence paid her by Germany.

Der Freischütz really belongs to the history of Romanticism. Here it must suffice to see Weber not only as a genius and a precursor, but as part of a developing tradition. Like Rossini, he was an innovator who effectively capitalized on possibilities in the work of lesser talents. Two of these had passed through Mannheim in earlier years; Georg Joseph Vogler (1749–1814), a sort of German Lesueur, eccentric theorist and teacher, evidently affected his pupil Weber's attitude to orchestral colour, while the Bohemian Franz Danzi (1763–1826), eminently orthodox in style, took Weber's works immediately into the repertory at Karlsruhe and himself took an interest in Romantic subject-matter. Peter Winter (1754–1825) was well known internationally, presenting operas in London (in Italian) and Paris, but he was most at home in the eclectic tradition of the *Singspiel*. He wrote a sequel to *The Magic Flute* (*Das Labyrinth*, text by Schikaneder, Vienna, 1798), but his most successful piece came two years earlier (*Das unterbrochene Opferfest*, also performed in Vienna). Joseph Weigl (1766–1846) contributed to various genres but showed most originality in charming domestic dramas; his *Die Schweizerfamilie* (Vienna, 1809), an appealing blend of folk-like lyricism and delicate colour, was widely performed throughout the nineteenth century. The pre-Romanticism of these works, like many from France and Italy, is, however, mitigated by their musical conservatism.

The critical year for German Romantic opera was 1816, when within a month E. T. A. Hoffmann's *Undine* (Berlin, 3 August) and Spohr's *Faust* (Prague, 1 September, directed by Weber) were first performed. Both are characterized by evocative orchestration, a tendency to break down the operatic form of discrete musical numbers by thematic cross-reference, and by their exploitation of supernatural menace within a naturalistic human society. Hoffmann's opera was the chief musical work of this inspired polymath, but it was little performed despite an appreciative review by Weber who learned from its delicate orchestration and the urgency of its dramatic presentation. Spohr's *Faust* is the work of a symphonist, and its historical significance lies partly in an elaborate system of recurring motives used less for musical ends than to assist the psychological development of the drama. The music, however, is in the end too much for the comparatively thin dramatic substance. Spohr's *Faust* has no connection with Goethe's tragically questing philosopher-hero, being rather more simply a man in thrall to a demon; but it points the way to such works as Meyerbeer's *Robert le diable* and Marschner's *Der Vampyr* as well as *Der Freischütz*. Spohr's next operatic successes were both oriental in setting: *Zemire und Azor* (1819), using the plot of Grétry's opera, and *Jessonda* (1822). The latter, another rescue of an oriental maiden by a European hero (cf *Oberon*), was a subject peculiarly well suited to the languid chromaticism and delicate orchestral blend of Spohr's post-Mozartean style.

Beethoven's debt to French opera referred only to one branch – the Cherubinian, Neoclassical and ethical – of its recent flowering. The Méhul, colouristic, proto-Romantic branch was of wider significance in the foundation of a distinctly national German opera. Most Germans would probably refer to *The Magic Flute* as prototype, but its philosophical dimension is hardly typical of early German Romanticism; in relation to the development of national opera its importance is no more, and no less, than that it is a masterpiece in German, a claim which could be lodged for the egregiously French *Fidelio*. When Weber took a stance against Italian domination, he accepted *Undine* and *Faust* as valuable precedents, but his most powerful ally was France. The main characteristics of *Der Freischütz* (Berlin, 1821) are those of *opéra comique*. The arias are direct in expression and free in form; a realistic rather than idealized pastoral setting is enhanced by melody which aspires to the condition of folksong, and by intoxicating orchestral colours, particularly for conjuring the supernatural. The chorus becomes the *Volk*; the principals are recognizably human types. Nearly all these elements derive from the structure and atmosphere of *opéra comique*.

None of this qualifies Weber's title to Romanticism, at least in opera. Unless, however, we take Hoffmann's definition of musical Romanticism and find it in Classical instrumental music, we need to seek for its origins in the songs and operas of France and Germany at the end of the eighteenth century, when literature and the visual arts were moving towards a Romantic vision. Musical history is a continuum which assimilates such movements; just as it passes, not unaffected but with surprising nonchalance, through the political and social minefields of the time. Opera of the early nineteenth century shows that changing tastes in subject-matter and musical style do not necessarily coincide. If intensity is an attribute of Romanticism, *La Vestale* and *Fidelio* are more Romantic than the Scott and Shakespeare operas of France and Italy, or than *Undine* and *Faust*. The significance of *Der Freischütz* is that subject and music share the same attributes to an unprecedented degree. More than Méhul, Hoffmann, or Spohr, Weber shows us the 'dark gods', and opera could never be the same again. Where the religion of *Fidelio* is the religion of Enlightenment, that of *Der Freischütz* is a religion of demons, and the principal character, Max, is a kind of bucolic Faust, tormented into the sin of despair and saved only by divine grace. When such matters become the essence of a vivid musical drama, a new wind is blowing, from quite another quarter than that which stirred the Enlightenment and its 'Classical' musical language.

CHAPTER TEN

Song

Solo singing in the later eighteenth century was not the exclusive province of opera. A stage career could be consolidated by appearance at public concerts; and singing was also an amateur activity. A substantial segment of the music-publishing industry depended on the marketing of material suitable for singing at home. The solo song was, accordingly, much cultivated, and if its artistic value seems relatively slight compared to its nineteenth-century descendant, its social importance was no less. Moreover when the German *Lied*, the French *mélodie*, and other sophisticated forms which flourished in the next century developed into one of our subtlest art-forms, they did so on a secure foundation in eighteenth-century song, rather as the string quartet developed symphonic potential on the basis of the divertimento.

By contrast with the international dominance of Italian opera and the widespread dissemination of Austro-Bohemian instrumental music, the solo song preserved local varieties of style and form. This is natural enough in a medium so intimately wedded to words. The social use of lyric poetry, in solo or polyphonic settings, is probably as old as civilization, and it continued to be cultivated despite the popularity of musical theatre. The repertories overlapped a good deal; borrowed tunes were the staple of improvised musical theatre and, conversely, operas no longer performed in the theatre survived in the form of favourite numbers, both in public concerts and the drawing-room.

Both these arenas displayed a healthy eclecticism, particularly in England where the pleasure gardens of London combined operatic excerpts with newly-composed items in operatic or simpler styles and, of course, with overtures and concertos. The gardens, so vividly evoked in contemporary illustrations and novels such as Fanny Burney's *Evelina* (1778), formed an almost classless recreation; and like the nineteenth-century Promenade concerts they catered musically for every taste. They were equally eclectic in their settings,

42 Vauxhall Gardens in 1736, showing the 'band pavilion' preceding the 'Moorish-Gothick' edifice, and several non-musical distractions.

the longest-lived garden, Vauxhall (1661–1859) boasting in 'Classical' times a 'Moorish-Gothick' pavilion for the orchestra. Most of the best musicians of the age worked in the gardens of Vauxhall and Ranelagh, although they had to compete with all kinds of other entertainments, sideshows, ballooning, fireworks and, not least, eating.

The English drawing-room musician is also familiar from novels. In families with servants, the daughter or niece of the house learned to sing, perhaps to a sister's accompaniment. Her repertory was usually rather simpler than that of Marionetta in Peacock's *Nightmare Abbey* (1818); besides singing a ballad, she makes allusion to operas by Paisiello, Rossini and Mozart. In Jane Austen's *Emma* (1816) the evasion of any playing by Mrs Elton, the obliging, musical, but technically suspect playing of Emma herself, and the exquisite performance of Jane Fairfax (who, although a gentlewoman, is destined to be a governess), symbolize their different characters and stations. And we are reminded in *Jane Eyre* that 'any English schoolgirl' could play a little, but that those of higher social strata could often play and sing well. Numerous manuscript or printed sources survive in the larger houses of England, containing music for amateurs in which celebrated melodies are set with simple, even rudimentary, accompaniment (for keyboard or harp); sometimes a straightforward instrumental part is provided, usually for flute. A late sample of such a compilation is Anne Brontë's Song Book, a manuscript of the early 1840s which includes crudely adapted music by Handel, Haydn and Mozart, as well as material purporting to be of folk origin.

Urban society also favoured convivial gatherings of men who would entertain themselves by singing. The catch, a form of round popular in England since the sixteenth century, maintained its hold, although bawdiness fell from fashion. The glee, originating in the seventeenth century, reached an artistic peak near the end of the eighteenth; it is a composition for male voices, usually in three parts, in a style which eschews intricacy. Among composers contributing to these forms were Webbe, Dibdin, S. Wesley, Pearsall and Richard Stevens (1757–1837), a collector of old music who composed several attractive glees to poems by Shakespeare. These composers and the glee movement in general are symptoms of English conservatism, which even after abandoning the Italianate madrigal remained faithful to an indigenous tradition of singing in parts.

Simpler forms of vocal music could be used for devotion as well as recreation. Although rare in Catholic parts of Germany and Austria (Haydn's *Gebet zu Gott* is an exception), the sacred song ('Geistliches Lied') had continued to flourish in the Protestant north during an era when solo song was at a generally low ebb. A more sophisticated artistic standard was introduced with C. P. E. Bach's 1758 publication of settings of Christian Gellert's collection of the previous year, *Geistliche Oden und Lieder*. These poems entered the Lutheran liturgy

43 *The Music Lesson* by J. H. Fragonard (1732–1806); art, flirtation and domesticity. Among Fragonard's work are illustrations from the repertory of *opéra comique.*

and some survive today as hymns; six of them were set as solo songs by Beethoven. No doubt it was the superior quality of Gellert's poetry which inspired not only the interest of major composers, but a more complex kind of music, and so contributed directly to the development of solo song in Germany.

Another contributory strand was one of the rediscoveries of folk music which have periodically fertilized the traditions of composed music. This was yet another field tilled by Rousseau, who notated songs in France and Italy (including Venetian gondoliers' songs); some appear in his *Consolations des misères de ma vie*, a collection of airs, duets and romances published posthumously in 1781. Folksong directly affected the principal vocal form of France, the romance, for which Rousseau, in his dictionary, prescribed above all simplicity, lack of ornament, and naivety. The romance was favoured by the middle classes, and survived the Revolution; its associations with earlier forms such as the *brunette*, and with folksong, became obscured, but it never lost touch with its origins in a pastoral conceit.

Similar interconnections of folk- and art-song arise throughout Europe. Folk music was still being created; some, although regarded as 'folk' because aurally transmitted, is of known authorship. Much Scottish fiddle music comes into this category, as do popular and satirical songs of the period such as Shield's *The Plough Boy* and, in Italy, operatic songs (Beethoven called 'Rule, Britannia' 'Volkslied' in the title of his variation set). The ballad form attracted serious poets, as did the most artless type of lyric. It soon became fashionable to publish folksongs in society clothes; the enterprising Edinburgh publisher George Thomson commissioned accompaniments, some-times for full piano trio, from, among others, Haydn, Pleyel, Beethoven and Weber.

In Germany, the simplicity of early settings of lyric verse, while it precludes them from being very interesting as music, does exemplify coherent principles. Goethe himself, like many hymn-writers and authors of ballad operas, wrote poetry to fit existing tunes, taking traditional as well as art-song for his model. His novel *Wilhelm Meisters Lehrjahre* (1795–6), and his plays *Egmont* and *Faust*, provided the best-loved texts of the next century. His ideal setting was largely syllabic, and in a strophic form to match that of the poetry. The melody should follow the verse rather than aspire to independence, and the accompaniment should not distract or even illustrate, except in the most general way. (German songs of the period were often written on two staves, the vocal melody being simply doubled). Nineteenth-century settings of Goethe's lyrics, starting with Schubert and Loewe, would have struck him as excessively musical.

In the development of vocal genres, most of the traffic was out of the theatre and into the concert or intimate gathering. The 'concert aria', of which Mozart was the greatest exponent, is at the opposite extreme of artificiality from the romance or ballad. Tailor-made for a particular singer, and often using an operatic text, these works are generally more broadly conceived than arias intended for the stage; they are celebrations of music and of singing, and are not dramatic even when they present a stylized image of drama in their recitatives. This music is among Mozart's most neglected, and is likely to remain so, not so much because the genre has no modern descendant as because the specificity of music to singer is so high that we are dealing almost with an esoteric art. When Mozart set Josepha Duschek a particular challenge with the leaping chromaticism of 'Bella mia fiamma' (K528, 1787), the point is clear, but the music is still uningratiating. An exception is the ravishing 'Ch'io mi scordi di te', with piano obbligato (K505, 1786). There is no reason to suppose Mozart was actually in love with Nancy Storace, the first Susanna, for whose farewell concert it was written, but the description of this limpid *rondò* as a musical love-letter remains strikingly apt.

When simple songs were imported into the theatre they were likely to acquire a full accompaniment and to be sung in an ornamented style. Everywhere, towards 1800, accompaniments developed independence, matching a greater variety of forms. In solo song the new instrument, the piano, still developing its range and volume, proved admirably suited to providing a subdued rhythmic continuum; eventually, in Schubert, it became equal in importance with the voice, conveying musical imagery absolutely crucial to the effect of the whole, and is in some cases more memorable than the voice part. Even in the French romance, the piano parts became fuller, with interludes, preludes and postludes, and the structure was no longer always strophic. With Martini's eternally popular *Plaisir d'amour* (1784), to a poem by the sentimental novelist and poet Florian, the gap between 'art' and 'folk-like' widened and the romance acquired the characteristics of the song-type later designated 'mélodie'. Strophic forms (usually of two verses) were familiar in

opéra comique, and a simplified romance type could be used to distinguish poems which would be sung even in a play, a famous example being Blondel's 'Une fièvre brulante' from Grétry's *Richard*. Major opera composers who cultivated the romance included Méhul, Boieldieu and Spontini.

Yet even in quite sophisticated romances the pastoral conceit remains. *Plaisir d'amour* was originally called *Romance of the Goatherd*, although its artificial melancholy is about as true to the realities of rural life as Marie Antoinette's full-sized toy farm at the Trianon. Berlioz's first published work (possibly from 1819, his sixteenth year) is *The spited shepherdess*, and its lilting rhythm and simple accompaniment are a young composer's homage to a familiar style. One of the earliest surviving manuscripts of Berlioz is a collection of romances with the accompaniments transcribed for guitar, for use in a community without a piano; songs of operatic origin are indistinguishable from the rest. But Berlioz's earliest original songs stretched the form beyond what was customary, and his settings of Thomas Moore (*Mélodies irlandaises*, 1829), and a ballad by Goethe, *Der Fischer* (less elaborately set by Schubert), bridge the gap between romance and high art, or 'mélodie'.

Parallel developments took place in Germany and, less momentously, in England. In Germany a significant stage is marked by the publication of Klopstock's collection of love-songs, *Oden* (1771). Within three years, seven of them had appeared in settings by Gluck, his only venture in this field; others followed, by Beethoven's

44 The 'Hamlet' at Trianon, Versailles, showing the false rusticity of the 'Lord's manor'.

45 Autographed title-page, with a note setting the scene as if for a staged performance, of Haydn's *Arianna a Naxos*, printed in London *c*. 1791.

teacher Neefe and, much later, by Schubert. Goethe's lyrics began to inspire musicians outside his immediate circle and uninhibited by his views on the subservience of music.

Mozart's first elaborate songs are in French (such as 'Dans un bois solitaire', composed at Mannheim in 1778), but his finest is Goethe's *Das Veilchen*, in which, despite the strophic structure of the poem, Mozart used a plan analogous to sonata form, perfectly matching the dramatic design and gentle irony of the poem. Haydn's contribution to German song was less significant than his remarkable sets of English Canzonettas, mainly to poems by Anne Hunter, and dating from his second London visit. They range from the sentimental strophic lyric 'My mother bids me bind my hair' to an intense, through-composed Shakespeare setting, 'She never told her love'. The piano writing of Haydn's sonatas and trios for the English instrument is evoked by the glitter of the *Mermaid's Song* and the powerful drive of *Fidelity*. A similar adventurousness can be found in a work composed for the Viennese piano, but which Haydn performed in England. The cantata *Arianna a Naxos* for voice and piano possesses a range of emotion and style comparable to opera; it is a true dramatic *scena* of the kind usually given orchestral support, equal in power to the fine orchestral *Scena di Berenice*, written for London in 1795.

Haydn's canzonets spawned a considerable progeny, including an English song by Beethoven (*La tiranna*, 1799). English song also derived stimulus from a new style of lyric poetry, in Byron, Scott,

Moore and Burns. Songs by Attwood, Pinto and John Clarke-Whitfield deserve a place at least on the fringes of the repertory, and set in train a gentle flowering of Romantic song which lasted throughout the nineteenth century. English poetry in translation, including Shakespeare as well as the moderns, contributed substantially to the literature available to German composers and was used by Schubert, Loewe and later Schumann.

The origins of German Romantic song are usually traced to the late eighteenth century. It is difficult, however, to see what Beethoven or Schubert can have learned from the syllabic type of setting, which adds little to the poetry except declamatory precision. Indeed, composers who started this way soon wearied of it and extended the piano accompaniments and postludes in which the composer, by having the last word, claims the poem for his own. More rarely, by a substantial introduction, the composer would arrogate to himself the right to cast an atmospheric spell, a vital step in imposing on the poem the single interpretation (or reading) which an 'art-song' necessarily is.

Goethe himself appreciated the work of his musical confidant Zelter (1758–1832), and of Reichardt (1752–1814), whose main claims to attention are, respectively, as Mendelssohn's teacher and as a major critic. Such simplistic affairs as Reichardt's setting of Goethe's ballad *Erlkönig* cannot be taken seriously in the light of what Loewe and Schubert made of the poem. Differentiation of the *dramatis personae* of the ballad is by dynamics (father, *forte*; son, *piano*) and by the Erlking being confined to one note; apart from a generalized movement given by the tempo and rhythm there is no musically generated atmosphere, not even the evocation of a galloping horse. So reticent a style has little to offer lyrics, let alone dramatic ballads. Yet the ballad was much in favour, as a form capable of a high artistic level without losing touch with its popular origin. For the composer the ballad poses a problem of length. *Erlkönig* is comparatively brief; Schubert's setting of Schiller's *Der Taucher* takes nearly half an hour. A ballad is a repetitive verse structure, and being a narrative it cannot be cut; but a strophic melody would be intolerable in so many repetitions. Moreover, if it involves a narrator a ballad cannot adopt a purely dramatic form. Despite operatic devices, notably obbligato recitative, and piano imitations of the orchestra, this problem was not really solved until Carl Loewe (1796–1869) made a speciality of ballads. The

158

model for the young Schubert was Zumsteeg (1760–1802), particularly in his harmonic adventurousness and choice of evocative piano figuration.

Greater variety of form and texture was admitted by Reichardt and Zelter in their later songs, perhaps after the model of *Das Veilchen* and Haydn's canzonets, which were soon translated into German. Beethoven in his formative years wrote songs in Italian, French and German, many of them demanding little more of his genius than his social pieces (canons and musical jests). His ability to reach beyond the norms of his time is shown in his setting of Matthison's *Adelaïde*, published in 1797, a *scena* which encompasses a remarkable variety of feeling within a sweeping melodic continuity.

Although they may appear slight beside his instrumental works or the songs of Schubert, Beethoven's songs constitute the first real *oeuvre* by a major composer in this field, and as such are a milestone in its history. His settings of Goethe were the yardsticks against which his successors measured their own. They include texts from *Faust* (*Song of the Flea*) and *Wilhelm Meister* ('Kennst du das Land'), and Klärchen's songs from *Egmont*, intended for stage performance. In the six Gellert songs (op. 48, *c.* 1801) Beethoven continued the hymn-like style of the previous century, mitigating the severe strophic form with piano variations in the last song. His most striking innovation was to run short songs together into a 'cycle'. *An die ferne Geliebte* (op. 98, 1816) is not the first *Liederkreis*, but it is the first major example, and among the most thoroughly integrated. The six songs play without a break. Taken individually they are simple in form, but the piano binds the cycle together by discreet variations within their repeated strophes, and by linking material. The last song returns decisively to the melody of the first. Although its delicate fragrance evokes the pastoral world of a bygone era, and its melodious style and subservient piano hardly go beyond what was normal at the time, *An die ferne Geliebte* remains one of Beethoven's most Romantic conceptions; its structural radicalism was ignored by Schubert and is unmatched even by Schumann.

Beethoven's songs, and the seventy or so by Weber, are part of a wide picture of developing interest in song-writing which capitalized on the flowering of Romantic lyric poetry early in the century and reached significant proportions in Poland and Bohemia (Tomášek's songs are in both Czech and German) as well as Britain, Germany and

46 *A Schubert Evening at Spaun's*: Moritz von Schwind's depiction of a 'Schubertiad'. The composer accompanies his first great interpreter, J. M. Vogl (1768–1840); Spaun is on Schubert's left.

Austria. But no composer before Hugo Wolf forged such an intimate relationship with song as Franz Peter Schubert (1797–1828). He possessed the advantages of training in voice and piano (he was also a string player), and benefitted from the ready accessibility of such models as Reichardt, Zumsteeg and Beethoven. Most important of all, he had access to the best new European poetry. His lively and intelligent circle of friends included poets (Johann Mayrhofer, Franz von Schober) as well as painters and dramatists whose social gatherings became known as 'Schubert evenings' or 'Schubertiads' and provided an intimate, critical audience for the prolific young composer.

Like any young artist, Schubert first attempted to master the prevailing genres; and nearly always, even when he appears clumsy, he transcends his models. His first ballad, *Hagars Klage*, written when he was fourteen, is overtly modelled on Zumsteeg. He tried his hand at Italian songs (like Beethoven, he studied with Salieri); he set many poems by eighteenth-century writers such as Klopstock and the elegant Matthison, including *Adelaïde*; he was long faithful to the

Neoclassical fantasies of Mayrhofer, and set many verses by Schiller. But the poet who first tapped the wells of genius in Schubert was Goethe. He would not have taken much pleasure in the fact, for Schubert's songs contravene every limitation he wished to impose on music – although in fairness to Goethe it must be said that his musical tastes developed and he greatly appreciated Beethoven's *Egmont*. Schubert's accomplishment, however, was nothing less than the annihilation of the poet; the song becomes not merely a possible reading of the poem but aspires to become the only one.

Song as a fully-fledged musical genre came of age with Schubert's setting of a *Faust* lyric, *Gretchen am Spinnrade*. *Gretchen* was composed in 1814, a year before *Erlkönig*, although it was the latter which Schubert, defying Goethe's bad opinion, published as op. 1 in 1821. Goethe's view of ballads, that they should be sung as ballads, not theatrically but as an oft-told tale whose very sadness gives comfort, is an objectification flouted by Schubert's *Erlkönig*, with its thundering hooves, its beguiling melody for the Erlking's seductions, above all its *verismo* wail of terror for the child; but because it embodies the horror of the tale, the music remains spellbinding after 150 years.

Gretchen am Spinnrade is a lyric within a drama, and is itself dramatic: Gretchen is voicing her own feelings. Goethe used verses

47 Schubert, *Gretchen am Spinnrade*; autograph (1814).

with short lines, as for Klärchen, to capture the unhappiness of a simple heart. Yet there is still a form of objectification in the perpetual motion of the spinning-wheel out of which Schubert fashions all but a few bars of the piano part. In a single inspiration he attained the quintessentially Schubertian song – an unbroken piano continuum, responding to the subtlest shifts in harmony, and a voice part which is neither simple declamation nor a clearly periodic melody. The harmony follows (or directs?) Gretchen's train of thought, wandering almost casually to unusual regions, only to return again to her obsession: 'My peace is fled, My heart is heavy'. As she thinks of Faust himself the accompaniment becomes less restless; then the harmony moves with frightening rapidity to her recollection of his kiss. The wheel falls still; after a harrowing pause it slowly picks up its original movement. The girl's despair now leads to a second intensification, with both the highest note in the voice and the inexorable reinforcement of the home key. In a final stroke not implied in Goethe, she begins the first verse again, but cannot complete it; and the wheel winds the song to a halt, so that we understand it finally as the symbolic embodiment of the girl's restless misery.

In thus equating the apparently objective and pictorial accompaniment with the central idea of the poem, Schubert raised art-song to an unprecedented level by means which owe little or nothing to any earlier composer. This achievement is matched, but never surpassed, in the field of Romantic song. The very intimacy of the medium lends it an intensity not possible in the inevitably more stylized form of opera – in which Schubert, despite many attempts, accomplished nothing of such enduring value as this, his first great song, written when he was seventeen.

CHAPTER ELEVEN

Instrumental music in the 'Age of Beethoven'

The conception of a composer's right not only to sell his work but to be an independent, creative spirit, is usually dated from Beethoven. In fact he was merely a stage in a continuing process of emancipation; too much can be made of his occasional boorishness towards his social superiors. Beethoven succeeded in holding the attention of Vienna, or at least of a small but influential group of supporters, perhaps because his rugged individualism marked him out as a man of destiny and hence a symbol of more general, and vaguely articulated, human yearnings. His position was presaged by Count Waldstein, who sent him to Vienna in 1792 to 'receive Mozart's spirit from Haydn's hands'. Patronage rarely failed Beethoven. His most generous supporter was his Imperial pupil Archduke Rudolph, whom in return Beethoven immortalized through the dedication of several works including the consummate *Archduke* Trio and the Mass in D.

Beethoven's success is part of a larger economic picture in which musicians could afford to specialize. His pupil Ferdinand Ries (1784–1838), a competent composer, made enough as a travelling pianist to retire at forty. He and Clementi were doubtless more prudent with their earnings than Clementi's pupil Field, who subsisted in Russia on fickle patronage, the sale of a few compositions, and the stale round of teaching; or Dussek, who abandoned his wife and debts in London (yet after a few more peripatetic years, he could afford to die of gout). There were still court posts in Germany. Spohr, despite his liberal leanings, was employed for most of his career by the petty absolutism of the court of Kassel. He came there, however, with a reputation earned, and was not punished for his frequent absences even when leave was arbitrarily withheld. The musical servant was by now an anachronism.

Many musicians before Beethoven lived without full-time employment. Mozart's failure, in the career-pattern in which Beethoven succeeded, indicates how Vienna lagged behind such centres as London and Paris in hospitality to independent artists.

Copyright developed slowly over this period; it was strongest in London, where J. C. Bach made case law by suing the publisher Longman in 1777. By the early nineteenth century the rights of an artist to his property were being established; composers could combine such sources of income as a part-time post, teaching, direct patronage, opera fees, sale of music, and performing, although few could shine in all these ways like Spohr. Beethoven, unfitted by deafness for a Kapellmeistership and performing, had to fight to take advantage of other possibilities; the result, fortunate for us, is that he devoted himself entirely to composition. He was not above hackwork, like the *Battle* Symphony and his cantata for the Congress of Vienna; but his serious works were competed for by German publishers and could be sold separately for publication in London. Even Schubert, confined to Vienna and proverbially impecunious, actually earned a useful sum in his last years, mainly from the sale of songs.

The travelling musicians, little affected by almost continual war until 1815, played not only in wealthy homes but, more prestigiously, in public concerts before the new middle-class audience. In Paris, London and the capitals of Germany concert societies developed rapidly, and some, like the Philharmonic Society in London, the

48 Miniature portrait of Beethoven in the year of the *Eroica* (1803), by C. Horneman.

Société des Concerts in Paris, and the Society of Friends of Music in Vienna, have a virtually unbroken history since their foundation. From the start Beethoven's symphonies were the central works of the repertory. Beethoven's supremacy may have discouraged other composers because such works could no longer be mass produced, and as a direct consequence the repertory began its slow atrophy. The Industrial Revolution brought with it an audience anxious to escape into a familiar dream; and the symphony without programmatic associations, allowing free rein to the imagination, in which Hoffmann found the most intense Romantic involvement, became a principal means of Romantic escapism.

OVERTURE AND CONCERTO

Beethoven's supremacy also encouraged diversification, including a revival of symphonic music with extra-musical connotations. The tendency to apply 'programmes' to Beethoven symphonies other than the *Pastoral* indicates an awareness of their singularity, and the *Pastoral* itself served to legitimize the trend. Beethoven provided further stimulus to extra-musical interpretation by his overtures. After 1800 the overture established itself as an independent genre. Operatic overtures were played in concerts, those which run straight into Act I, like some of Gluck's and *Don Giovanni*, being furnished with concert endings. Most overtures had less connection with the opera they preceded, and their adaptation of symphonic first-movement form, or alternatively their easy-going sectional form (Rossini's *William Tell*), made them agreeable concert items. Some were composed for concert use, with or without a poetic title. Spohr used the term 'Grand Concert Overture'; others contributing to the genre of concert overture without a subject were Reicha, Cherubini, Mendelssohn (the *Trumpet* overture) and Schubert, who composed two overtures 'in the Italian style' in 1817.

Concert overtures with a subject took their lead from such works as Beethoven's *Coriolan*. This was written in 1807 for a play by Collin, but possibly not used in the theatre; the 'programme', never explicit, may have seemed to justify its unusual structure. In the equally popular *Egmont* overture, part of the music for Goethe's drama, the brilliant conclusion is unrelated to the rest of the overture, and can only be justified programmatically. (Beethoven used the same music at the end of the play, for which Goethe required a 'Symphony of Victory'.) But he used the same gesture, an unexpected change to the major and a faster tempo, at the end of the quartet op. 95, in F minor, the same key as *Egmont*, and written the same year, 1810. The four overtures to *Fidelio/Leonore* also enriched the repertory, and with these and the opera overtures of Weber and Cherubini as models, composers wrote poetically inspired concert overtures which form the pre-history of the symphonic poem. From 1826 come Mendelssohn's concert overture *A Midsummer Night's Dream* (the incidental music followed much later), and Berlioz's first overture, *Les francs-juges*, both soon to become popular in concerts. In the next few years the Shakespearian overture became fashionable, although none encapsulates the characters and development of the play within a lucid form as well as Mendelssohn in his precocious masterpiece.

The use of programmes, and the use of solo instruments, are both calculated to appeal to an audience impatient of complexity but eager for the unusual. A soloist has inherent dramatic potential, which hardly requires programmatic assistance; nevertheless the *locus classicus* of 'solo versus orchestra', the slow movement of Beethoven's Fourth Piano Concerto, recalls to many listeners Gluck's Orpheus taming the Furies. Natural and military scenes were popular; Field's fifth concerto is called *L'incendie par l'orage* (1817). The hunt lends itself to musical treatment in piano pieces by Clementi and Dussek, and in Méhul's popular overture *La chasse du jeune Henri*. Spohr, four of whose later symphonies are programmatic, wrote his eighth violin concerto (1820) *in modo di scena cantante*, a plotless dramatic cantata. Weber's most original solo work is his *Konzertstück* for piano (1821, a decade later than his concertos). Weber acknowledged the programme only in private, but it controls the highly original musical structure. The mediaeval lady mourns the absence of her Crusading husband (slow and fast 'pathetic' styles); a March signals his return and the scintillating finale is their rapturous reunion.

The supreme masterpiece of Classical programme music is Beethoven's Sixth Symphony, the *Pastoral* (1808). Seeing Nature with the idealism of the previous century, Beethoven adhered to a more modern aesthetic in claiming the work to be 'more the expression of feeling than painting'. The feeling, however, is objectified, and the brook, birdsong, roistering peasants, and thunderstorm are as literally 'painted' as in Haydn's *The Seasons*. The final movement, 'Thanksgiving after the storm', restores to feeling the primacy it otherwise enjoys only in the first movement, and its rainbow beauty indicates that feeling and painting are in any case compatible. The *Pastoral* is the summation of music's response to an ideal vision of country life before the Agricultural Revolution. If it is programmatic, it is in the picturesque, not the dramatic, vein; if it looks ahead it is to the *Spring* and *Italian* symphonies rather than the *Fantastique* and *Manfred*.

Beethoven's determination to avoid routine means that successive works are almost wilfully unalike. The Fourth Symphony (1806) seems, after the *Eroica*, to retrench, its only formal innovation being a multiplication of the scherzo-trio ABA to ABABA; its overall form, with a light finale, harks back to Haydn. The haunting Adagio, the electric tempi and dynamics of the fast movements, and some remarkable tonal adventure in the first Allegro, make this no Neoclassical exercise. Beethoven further consolidated his symphonic achievement in the quartets of 1805–6 (op. 59), known as 'Rasumovsky' after their dedicatee, the Russian ambassador; the first two incorporate Russian melodies. These quartets are chamber music without intimacy, compressed symphonies. No. 1 in F major is the *Eroica* of quartet literature, particularly in its long and densely argued first movement, and its slow movement, a heartrending elegy. The Scherzo is unique, its structure without repetitions bearing no resemblance to the conventional form of such movements and allowing a scale of operations comparable to a first movement. The other two op. 59 quartets may be less radical, but debts to the past are repaid with interest. For example, the finale of no. 3 emulates Mozart's integration of fugue with sonata form in K387, but it is a power-driven movement totally foreign to Mozart's aesthetic.

Beethoven broke new ground with the great *Leonora* overtures, and their dramatization of the yielding of darkness to light through heroic endeavour suggested properties which could be turned to musical ends. The design of the Fifth Symphony is weighted heavily towards its ending, not in intensity (even Beethoven is seldom more intense than in the first movement) but in length and loudness, helped by an expanded orchestra. Beethoven's Fifth has probably been more argued over than any other of his symphonies except the Ninth, for it so clearly embodies *meaning*, and insistently demands explanation in terms beyond those which describe its structure. The furious but controlled energy of the first movement, breaking off at the reprise for a plaintive oboe solo; the triumphant glow of the trumpets intruding upon the elaborate variations of the second movement; the demonic Scherzo and sinister bridge into the finale; the inescapable motivic connections of first movement and Scherzo; the recurrence of the Scherzo during the finale; to this concatenation of strange (if not unprecedented) events Beethoven provides no real clue. Early commentators like Hoffmann and Berlioz, who responded to its originality and power rather than its equally impressive architectural properties, naturally considered it the embodiment of artistic liberation.

Again, Beethoven seemed to retrench, his next radical expansion of the symphony being no. 9 (see chapter 12). No. 7 in A (1812–13) is an internal transformation of the genre, its character well expressed by Wagner, who called it 'the apotheosis of dance'. The graver measure, however, is not trodden by a Neoclassical minuet – there is a quicksilver scherzo instead – but by the Allegretto slow movement. This is a rare case of complete agreement between the public and the musical connoisseur; not only did it become so popular that it replaced the legitimate slow movement of the Second Symphony, it also profoundly affected the next generation of composers, among those paying it the sincerest form of flattery being Schubert, Berlioz and Mendelssohn. The Romantics favoured the odd-numbered Beethoven symphonies; no. 8 in F, composed at the same time as no. 7, appears almost a miniature until the finale broadens out by means of a tonal time-bomb which explodes in the coda. No. 8 is a refreshingly subversive work in relation to a view of Beethoven which sees him progressing from the post-Classical to the sublime.

Other symphonists working in Beethoven's lifetime continued either in ignorance of or in conscious dispute with Beethoven's boldness. Several isolated works merit attention, including the single symphonies of two composers who died young, the Bohemian Voříšek (1791–1825) and the Spaniard Arriaga (1806–26). Mendelssohn's first orchestral symphony, in C minor, dates from 1824. Clementi wrote symphonies for London between 1812 and

1824; another Bohemian, Jan Václav Kalliwoda (1801–66) and the Englishman Cipriani Potter (1792–1871) continued in the vein of early- to middle-period Beethoven in their short series of symphonies. Potter's talent was acknowledged by Beethoven; he later became principal of London's first great music college, the Royal Academy (founded in 1822), and his G minor symphony was revived as late as 1855, when it was conducted by Wagner.

The opposite pole of attraction to Beethoven, and a composer widely regarded as his equal, was Ludwig Spohr (1784–1859), three of whose ten symphonies were written before 1830. Spohr was quite uninhibited by Beethoven, for whom his admiration was severely qualified. Himself a master of suave chromaticism, he found Beethoven harsh, particularly the Fifth Symphony: 'It has many beauties, but they do not add up to a classical whole. The very first theme, in particular, lacks the dignity essential to the opening of a symphony.' Spohr hankered after the purer air of Mozart, and his passion for order was such that he divided his string quartets into concerto-like 'Quatuors brillants' and true quartets, discourses among equals. Spohr was the most consistently successful serious composer of his day, and his music merits careful revaluation, but it is likely that its ingratiating fluency will continue to be inimical to his reputation.

Spohr wrote chamber music for all combinations, and in one at least he followed Beethoven's lead with conspicuous success. This was the compressed orchestra of Beethoven's Septet, of whose concertante violin part he presumably approved. Spohr composed a delightful octet, including variations on Handel's 'Harmonious Blacksmith', for clarinet, two horns, violin, two violas, cello and bass; and a nonet for one of each string and wind. This kind of group forms an interesting sub-genre, with works by Clementi and the prolific Franco-British Georges Onslow, an attractive septet by the Swede Franz Berwald (1829), and one crowning masterpiece, Schubert's Octet (1824). Spohr also extended groups of strings to eight players in a double quartet; it is his misfortune to have been outfaced by Mendelssohn's precocious Octet of 1825.

Apart from large-scale 'Harmoniemusik', wind chamber music was growing in popularity; the wind quintet (flute, oboe, clarinet, horn, bassoon) became standardized and its repertory was founded on nearly thirty works by Reicha. Chamber music with piano, however, was more cultivated, and more suited to a pre-Romantic idiom based on richness of harmony and texture. Both Hoffmann and Spohr contributed to this genre, a favourite medium being the piano quartet. Particularly attractive are works by Frederick II's nephew, admired as a composer by Beethoven and Weber. A charismatic soldier, Louis Ferdinand of Prussia (1772–1806) fell in battle against Napoleon. He deserved Schumann's epithet, 'a Romantic among Classicists'; his blend of delicate expressiveness, liveliness and technical expertise can be enjoyed in his piano quartets and a luscious octet for clarinet, two horns, two violas, two cellos and piano. His untimely end inspired a heartfelt sonata, the 'Harmonic Elegy' in F sharp minor, from his teacher Dussek.

VIRTUOSITY AND THE PIANO

The early years of the nineteenth century are not least remarkable for the growth of instrumental virtuosity. A period of rapid development in the capabilities of the piano, brass and the clarinet, it was inevitably also a period of rapid obsolescence as virtuoso–composers were tempted by fame and fortune into writing works with more show than substance. It takes more than usual historical insight, including a knowledge of the state of the instruments' development, to appreciate the novelty, and the sheer joy of virtuosity, in much of this music. Virtuosity may also isolate the artist, setting him apart as magician or charlatan, surrounding him with a Romantic or (in the case of Paganini) saturnine aura. The foundations of Liszt's transcendental virtuosity lie in this period of Dussek, Weber, Field and Hummel; and the unbroken continuity of the post-Classical and Romantic piano schools will be clear when it is pointed out that Chopin had written six works for piano and orchestra by 1831 (the year of Mendelssohn's first mature piano concerto).

Mozart's delicate balance of solo and orchestra, preserved in Beethoven's overtly symphonic type of concerto, was of no interest to Chopin. His principal models (whose final works for piano and orchestra were not performed until after 1831) were friendly rivals for public esteem, Hummel and the expatriate Irishman John Field (1782–1837). Like Hummel, Field began in a Classicistic vein; he was, after all, Clementi's apprentice. His seven concertos, written between

1799 and 1832, vie in brilliance and ornamental elegance with the art of the operatic prima donna. The orchestra is completely subservient, and he was often moved, in concerts, to perform the concertos by himself, losing contrast in the fast movements but very little in the sensitive, nocturnal slow movements.

Field's reputation was the more remarkable in that he seldom travelled. The normal pattern was the mobility of Hummel, Ries, or Ignaz Moscheles (1794–1870), well known as a friend of Mendelssohn and Schumann and with five concertos to his credit before 1830. Violinists joined the circuit of travelling virtuosi, and the trail blazed by Viotti (1755–1824) was followed with success by Spohr and sensationally by Paganini (1782–1840), a legend in his lifetime, whose concertos and caprices are still among the hardest violin music ever composed. Spohr wrote twelve violin concertos before 1830, and four for the clarinettist Hermstedt. Crusell, his own interpreter, and Weber, collaborating with Bärmann, enlarged the repertory for this most versatile of wind instruments. Weber's operatically oriented manner makes particularly effective the singing tone, wide range, and registral contrast of the clarinet, for which he composed two concertos, a Grand Duo Concertant with piano, a concertante quintet, and a single-movement concertino.

While the concerto was the principal public form for the virtuoso, the solo recital was gaining ground in the heyday of Dussek and Steibelt. If we omit Beethoven and Schubert, who were atypical, the piano music of the early nineteenth century presents a richly varied scene in which technical brilliance was balanced by an almost equally extravagant sensibility – not the expressive intimacy of 'Emp-findsamkeit' but the heart-on-sleeve emotionalism of opera. A few composers continued to cultivate the sonata – a fine example is Voříšek's last major work, in B flat minor – but others, such as the mature Field, neglected it.

Indeed, by the 1820s the sonata was scarcely in fashion even from so respected a figure as Clementi. His experiments with it include an evocative (rather than programmatic) G minor sonata entitled *Didone abbandonata*, and a Capriccio in C which opens in quintuple metre and whose principal Allegro is in B minor. Admirable, as well as quirky, inventions are, however, spoiled by a tendency to prolixity common in this period, when Beethoven's concentration was little understood. A Classical limpidity is restored in Hummel's late sonata in D (1824);

and Weber's last sonata, in E minor (1822), strikes a new balance between lyricism and intensity. Its opening is no longer frenzied, but is an unaccompanied melodic line whose spaciousness justifies, for once, the length of what follows. Here, and in Schubert's late sonatas, the post-Classical style finds equilibrium.

A development in this period which lacks the sonata's ancestry, but which is of more importance for Romanticism, is the short piano piece; no longer a dance movement but either a virtuosic work which subdues architecture to the display of some particular technical facility, or a vignette suited to self-communing by amateur pianists. The piano study, as distinct from the technical exercise without musical content, had its origin in Clementi's idea of a published work combining pedagogical with musical value. To his irritation, he was anticipated by the first set of forty-two studies published in 1804 by J. B. Cramer (1771–1858). Cramer's studies were widely used and imitated (Beethoven's annotations to twenty-one of them have recently been published), and they inaugurated a fashion for such sets, usually of twelve or of twenty-four in all keys (such as those of Hummel, Kalkbrenner (twice), and Cipriani Potter). Cramer's conception of the study, treating a technical problem but also forming a rounded, even expressive, musical statement, culminated in Chopin's two sets, the first (op. 10) begun in 1829. Clementi finally published his *Gradus ad Parnassum* in 1817, a compendium of pieces including technical exercises, sonata movements, fugues, and pieces of no preconceived design, many of them among his best music.

Václav Tomášek (1774–1850) published sets of six piano pieces (1807–19) with the Virgilian title *Eclogues*. Paradoxically, this reference to the most Classical of poets is itself premonitory of Romanticism, although the attractive material is firmly ordered on a ternary plan like a minuet and trio. Beethoven's Bagatelles span most of his working life, and were selectively published in sets (op. 33 in 1802, op. 119 in 1822, and op. 126 two years later). They possess the subtlest balance of almost any music between a sense of completeness and of improvisatory fragmentation. Some appear to be large ideas treated elliptically; others present self-contained ideas without elaboration. The naivety is only apparent; Beethoven ordered the sets with care, omitting pieces which did not fit (some, like 'Für Elise', were only published posthumously). Here, perhaps, is the source of Schumann's disparate, yet integrated, piano cycles. Schubert's main contribution to the short piano piece consists of eleven Impromptus and six *Moments Musicaux*, deservedly beloved of amateur and concert pianists alike.

One of the *Moments Musicaux*, in C sharp minor, perhaps fortuitously illustrates an important new factor in keyboard music of this period, for its texture strikingly resembles the perpetual figuration of a Bach prelude. Bach was 'in the air'; the first publications of the '48' came out at the turn of the century. Beethoven's overt homage, in the extended fugal writing of his last works, is another facet of this 'Bach revival', but more forward-looking is the use of continuous figuration with minimal cadential articulation, thereby undoing the basis of *galant* style. An early and splendid example is Dussek's *Harmonic Elegy* for Louis Ferdinand; the restless syncopation of its finale comes close to the language of Schumann. The study often uses a texture of perpetual motion by concentrating on a single technique. At the same time, however, the growing ability of the piano to create an impression of sustained, even singing, tone (cantabile) gave rise to textures which continued to favour periodic melody with accompaniment, like an aria: left-hand arpeggios, held by the open pedal, support a simple melodic structure capable of bearing ornament. The 'Nocturne', which was the invention of Field, is the genre most closely associated with this pianistic texture, but it is also encountered in Hummel and occasionally Beethoven himself, notably in his Fourth Piano Concerto and the Adagio of the *Hammerklavier* sonata op. 106.

SCHUBERT

The only composer whose symphonies survive comparison with Beethoven is Schubert, not in the six written before he was twenty-one, but in two masterpieces, one unfinished. The first six evoke Haydn and also Rossini, notably the tarantella finale of no. 3. Schubert's interest in Beethoven was concentrated to a remarkable extent on the Second Symphony, which is almost quoted in the second movement of Schubert's symphonic piano duet, the Grand Duo (1824). Schubert's Seventh Symphony in E is a full-length draft which he never filled out; but his Eighth in B minor is the one invariably known as *Unfinished*. It consists of two movements of wonderful quality, complete in every way, followed by a

49 Schubert, the only page completed in score of the Scherzo of his *Unfinished* Symphony (no. 8 in B minor); autograph (1822).

fragmentary Scherzo (there is also a fine piano sonata in C with two complete movements). Here, in 1822, Schubert made the orchestra entirely his own. The whispering opening – written before he can have known Beethoven's Ninth – and mournful cantabile of clarinet and oboe, with a still more doleful horn echo, must suffice as an example of this work's haunting poetry.

In 1824 Schubert embarked on a campaign in which he set out to emulate Beethoven; he would write three string quartets, then a grand symphony. The quartets were the luminous and lyrical work in A minor; the D minor, called *Death and the Maiden* because the slow movement takes this song as theme for variations; and the stupendous G major quartet, not finished until 1826. In structure and texture these works are not in the least like Beethoven, but in scale they match the Rasumovsky quartets. Their expansiveness results less from symphonic drive than from an insouciant but entirely successful spinning out, by prolonged melodic paragraphs, massive dramatic transitions, and large-scale repetition and sequence. In these respects

Schubert the master of song put the Classicistic instrumental style into a lyrically induced overdrive and prepared himself for the symphony on the scale of the *Eroica* which followed. The 'Great' C major (composed almost certainly in 1825 but possibly revised later) is one of the most original works in symphonic literature, and it is not surprising that it could not be performed in Schubert's lifetime or for some time afterwards; recalcitrant instrumentalists refused to take it seriously because of the interminable reiteration of accompanimental motifs. Schubert abandoned traditional dialectic for ebullient rhythms and lyrical paragraphs of unprecedented sweep, and found an orchestral idiom to match. Schumann referred equivocally to the Andante's 'heavenly length'; Bernard Shaw called the symphony brainless. The songwriter's symphony *par excellence*, on its own terms it beggars criticism.

Schubert's last contributions to instrumental music, following the delightful but prolix piano trios, came from 1828, at the end of which year he died. They include the marvellous Fantasia in F minor for piano duet and the quintet with two cellos in C major, another very long work which, after the rampageous G major quartet, restores to Schubert's chamber music a Mozartean serenity, in that its drama and lyricism are tempered by a renewed control of musical architecture. The same can be said of his last complete instrumental works, the three piano sonatas of 1828. Schubert's persistent cultivation of this form is an indication of his indifference to fashion. He began with a profusion of works, which tend to lapse into Italianate lyricism, about 1817–19; those with most originality of texture, such as the one in F minor, are often unfinished. A marked tautening of design appears in two splendid sonatas in A minor of 1823 and 1825, which begin the mature series. The G major sonata of 1826 is almost excessively serene and expansive; it was entitled 'fantasia' by a fashion-conscious publisher, but it and the capricious sonata in D of the same year are fully in accordance with Schubert's sonata aesthetic.

In his last months Schubert carefully sketched and completed three grand sonatas with the intention of dedicating them to the greatest surviving master of the form, Hummel. These works, a worthy end to his instrumental output, sum up many facets of his style. The A major develops its first idea so freely on the first page that the usual order of exposition–development is virtually reversed, the central part of the movement being almost motionless. The slow movement is a barely coherent improvisation, recapturing the mood of the astonishing *Wanderer* Fantasia of 1822; the finale is a leisurely rondo on a Beethovenian pattern (Beethoven's loveliest example, Schubertian *avant la lettre*, is in op. 90). The finest slow movements are those of the C minor sonata (in Schubert's favourite five-part form, ABABA, with increasingly elaborate figuration) and the B flat sonata which recaptures the timeless quality of the C major quintet. The C minor sonata is like a last outburst of *Sturm und Drang*, while the B flat is a masterpiece of deceptive leisureliness, its huge paragraphs encompassing a subtle drama of theme and key.

These superb works complete Schubert's successful campaign to reconcile Classic proportions with his own lyrical expansiveness. The balance is delicate, and can be ruined by insensitive performance, for Schubert's time-scale involves extremely rapid harmonic change as well as prolonged static areas. One can only guess at the sequel, had Schubert lived a normal span. In his last few days he began a symphony of which the sketches suggest new paths; but 'no. 10' is too fragmentary, even in Brian Newbould's sensitive realization, to be considered canonical. The inheritors of his late instrumental style belonged to a much later generation: Brahms, Bruckner and Mahler, for whom Schubert provided an alternative to the obvious model of symphonic idealism. The fact would have surprised this modest idolizer of Beethoven, obscure in his own quarter of 'Biedermeyer' Vienna.

CHAPTER TWELVE

Epilogue: late Beethoven

'Classical' music began under the *ancien régime* but flourished partly thanks to middle-class wealth. It merged into 'Romanticism' with the old autocracies in decline and the capitalist and imperialist nation-state in the ascendant. Since society is a consumer of music, such changes in the social, economic and political ordering of the Western world inevitably affected musicians and musical composition. The late works of Beethoven are particularly valuable to an understanding both of the force and the limitations of such external influences.

Beethoven is a potent symbol because he succeeded as a freelance composer without being in any sense popular. Most of his predecessors – J. C. Bach is a good example – wrote in order to delight without effort, and aimed their music at a discernible market which would be equally receptive to any number of other composers. C. P. E. Bach and Haydn could afford experiments because they were in steady employment. Mozart, however, in his piano quartets and quintets, tried to carve out a market for himself, and failed; his quintets were not readily played or understood by the amateur and they were not interchangeable with anyone else's precisely because of the qualities which lead us to value them above those of Boccherini. Beethoven's music was still more difficult, and he wrote still less in the saleable and popular genres. Instrumental music more complex than its social context required was not new; it extends back beyond Haydn's *Sturm und Drang* to C. P. E. Bach, and perhaps farther. For Beethoven, however, difficult and demanding instrumental music came to predominate in his output as it never did in Haydn's, Mozart's or Schubert's.

Social change may have been a prerequisite of Beethoven's survival. But to 'explain' Beethoven's existence we can only invoke something élitist in a society increasingly egalitarian, something irrational in a society of growing scientific knowledge and industrial skill: the statistically improbable and Romantic concept of genius. Beethoven, with all the talent to be popular, persisted in being difficult and in raising difficulties for himself. In his late twenties, already a successful composer and virtuoso, he devoted himself to the strictest contrapuntal discipline; later, as his sketches show, he made composition a labour where it could have been easy. His objective seems to have been permanence, through perfect control of his own originality. He is the counterpoise to the collective Classical style promulgated by Ratner, and the final argument for Rosen's concept of Classicism as the achievement of a few; beyond the superficial similarity of language required to be comprehensible, Haydn, Mozart and Beethoven actively rejected the saleable symmetries of the *lingua franca*.

Beethoven's last quartets descend linearly from the mid-eighteenth-century *divertimento a quattro*, but they are different in kind, just as his Mass in D is different in kind from a liturgical *missa brevis* and his Ninth Symphony from an operatic sinfonia. In terms of a Classic-Romantic antithesis, he is a paradox; his language is founded in the Classical eighteenth century but his works appeal by their uniqueness as Romantic. But Beethoven beggars such petty distinctions as much as he scorns accountability in terms of extra-musical forces.

We should not exaggerate the isolation of Beethoven at the end of his life. Chamber music was not entirely out of fashion; Spohr and Onslow were particularly active in exploring new string textures, as was Mendelssohn, whose beautiful quartet in A op. 13 (1827) is partly a response to Beethoven's op. 95, while in other respects, notably the use of a song as introduction, it speaks the language of Romanticism. In the 1830s the aging Cherubini finished a set of quartets which would not have seemed out of place in Haydn's Austria but which appeared in a France generally unsympathetic to such music – a curious epilogue to a repertory whose true finale is Beethoven. All these works are worth study for their own sake and only appear traditional if we regard late Beethoven and Schubert as representative. Schubert, however, despite his youth, was as much possessed by a demon as Beethoven, and must be considered his equal in eccentricity.

Beethoven's eccentricity cannot be blamed on his deafness. If he was ever totally without hearing, it was at most for his final decade, and his compositional grounding was settled before he even became aware of his illness. Nor was he isolated from recent developments, being aware of Weber's *Der Freischütz*, of Spohr and Rossini, if not of Schubert. His reputation, and his patrons, allowed him the liberty to labour long at individual works and shape them as he pleased; accordingly his last works are as few in number as they are large with significance. In a period of prolific composers Beethoven's last decade produced little more than one mass, one symphony, a set of piano variations, and handfuls of sonatas and quartets; for most composers in full flight, three or four years' work at most. (Many high opus numbers are more or less arbitrarily assigned to belatedly published early works, such as the Octet op. 103, written in 1793.)

The phenomenon of 'late Beethoven' has cast a shadow over all subsequent work in the same genres. In this distillation of a genius who considered his *Pastoral* to be more feeling than imitation, the final abandonment of conventional frameworks and increasing concentration on the monochrome piano and string quartet tend to repel easy enjoyment; the music is all intellect, all feeling, and hence, to many musicians, went near to or beyond the limits of intelligibility. A mind clear of expectation, other than that aroused by the music itself, may for the same reasons (the absence of empty gestures, of transitional padding, of display) come to agree with Bernard Shaw who found the late quartets far easier than the symphonic op. 59. Where nothing is included not germane to the discourse, historical exegesis becomes superfluous; the music exists of and for itself and the musical listener.

The beginnings of 'late' Beethoven cannot be chronologically determined. The *Archduke* Trio (1810) may seem archetypically middle-period in its noble breadth, but the F minor quartet of the same year is one of his most elliptical works. Beethoven often wrote works in pairs, but his twins are never identical (the Fifth and Sixth symphonies are the obvious example). The massive proportions of the piano sonata op. 106 (1817–18) cannot disguise its 'late' essence, while the delicacy of the violin sonata op. 96 (1812–15) might seem 'late' had it not been anticipated, for instance in the F sharp major piano sonata op. 78 (1809). The cello sonatas op. 102 (1815) are a turning-point, for they still seem wilful today, while the piano sonata in A op. 101 of the following year, equally strange in design – a short Allegretto, an ironic march in F, an incomplete Adagio, a snatch of

50 Beethoven, the first page of his last piano sonata (op. 111 in C minor); autograph (1822).

the Allegretto leading to a huge finale – forms a miraculously harmonious whole.

Such higher harmony – usually termed 'unity' – is thereafter ever-present despite the diversity of musical ideas in all the late works. In particular, Beethoven's lifelong interest in variation form and in counterpoint reaches a new flowering, with a consequent reduction in sonata forms. This does not mean that Beethoven recognized the exhaustion of the Classical sonata style. It implies a unique renewal of it, for Beethoven informed variations and fugue with the spirit of the sonata, and the sonata with the spirit of variations and fugue. Stylization, so important to the eighteenth century, is unnecessary in music which refers so intensely to itself; the dialectic of comprehensibility is no longer carried on against a background of other music, but only of Beethoven's own. The interdependence of the late quartets is a familiar topic, especially the central three (op. 130 in B flat, op. 131 in C sharp minor, and op. 132 in A minor). But it is no less important in the last five piano sonatas, which shed light on one another's individuality. Consider the finales: fugal development (op. 101) precedes full-scale fugue (op. 106); a fugal variation (op. 109) prepares for the variation of a fugue (op. 110); a variation set in which contrast is a forming principle (op. 109) complements another in which similarity guides the ear through a gradual acceleration of note-values (op. 111). The minor-key slow movement, cut off short in op. 101, grows immense in op. 106. Op. 109 and op. 110 use minor keys for their fastest movements, but op. 110 brings back a minor-key slow movement as well, the *arioso dolente* which precedes the fugue. Op. 110 begins almost as another variation in the serene triple metre of the finale of op. 109. Variations reach an apotheosis in the Diabelli set, op. 120; its lively waltz theme possesses significant elements in common with the *arietta* theme of the variations in op. 111. The Diabelli Variations are also patterned by pairings of similarity and contrast, of departure from elements of the theme and return. These can be compared with the dialectic of a sonata; and the set includes a splendid fugue before the last, strict variation in which the vulgar waltz is transmuted into a stately, ornate minuet.

These piano works were written between 1816 and 1822. Before the more concentrated work on the five quartets (1823–6) Beethoven turned his attention to completing two huge projects. Inner harmony is less evident in the Mass in D (*Missa solemnis*, finished 1823) and Ninth Symphony (finished 1824), but with these public genres the criteria for a critical assessment must be different. Beethoven took his greatest creative risk when he rejected workings for an instrumental finale for the Ninth in favour of an immense movement, very difficult to perform, for soloists and chorus with orchestra. The Ninth was a triumph at its first performance, perhaps aided by the presence in the same programme of choral 'Hymns' (actually sections of the Mass in D, retitled because liturgical music was not allowed in the theatre). Ever since, however, it has seemed problematic to many listeners and to music criticism.

Perhaps such a work should not be accepted too easily. There is much, of course, to enjoy in the pure but adventurous symphonic idiom: the magical scherzo fugato, roughly interrupted by timpani, the ornate variations of the slow movement, the rugged first movement with its terrifying crescendo beside which Rossini's crescendos are playthings. Then, in an attempt to unify the work, Beethoven resorts to a desperate – which is not to say necessarily unsuccessful – ploy, bringing back snatches of earlier movements in response to a wandering recitative 'in search of a theme'. Once found, the noble melody is varied, then after a third grinding interruption the voices enter with the implication that instrumental music, the finest achievement of the last fifty years, is still inadequate.

The finale can be understood as a musical form, and needs to be, for its structure does not depend on the few verses of Schiller's *Ode to Joy* which Beethoven actually used. It is almost a complete symphony in itself: first variations, then scherzo (the march, a variation and fugal development), slow movement ('Be embraced, O ye millions') with a new motive, and finale combining the variation and slow movement themes in double fugue, with peroration and coda. The form is not unlike Schubert's *Wanderer* Fantasia, written in ignorance of the Beethoven (in 1822) and a seminal work for the formal inventions of Liszt. The problem of the Ninth's finale is not its form but its message, which demanded of Beethoven a simplicity, even banality, which might seem at odds with the complexity of the form. A sequence of moods like that of the Fifth Symphony lies behind the whole work: a grim first movement, a sinister dance, hymn-like slow movement, and ultimately optimistic finale. The problem, no doubt, is ours, in that such confidence, even achieved after a terrible struggle, may now seem misplaced; Thomas Mann's *Dr Faustus* made one of his final achievements to 'take back' the Ninth. But the world would be poorer if, while unable to share it, we did not acknowledge the value of such idealism.

The Mass, completed at the same time, is less problematic in that it is all vocal, and employs a traditional text. Beethoven may not have practised his religion conventionally, but he studied the Ordinary of the Mass deeply and his intensity of response makes enormous demands on the listener. Even where there remains a conventional formal response, as in the use of fugue at 'Et vitam venturi', it strikes freshly, as well as outdoing its models in immensity and power; and the insertion of slow, rapturous solo music before the end draws the strict style into something like a divine revelation. As in the march of the Ninth's finale, there is a risk of literalness in the blessing of the solo violin (Benedictus) and the military sounds at 'Dona nobis pacem'; in this 'Prayer for inner and outer peace' the externals, including the agonized prayer in recitative, are in danger of swamping the inwardness. These risks, however, are integral to the greatness of

Beethoven's last public works; they would be diminished if they were less aesthetically discomforting.

The last quartets are not open to such equivocation. They still contain problems for the critic and listener, but they should not be considered esoteric works accessible only to a cultivated initiate. The three in major keys (op. 127 in E flat, op. 130 in B flat, and op. 135 in F) are full of humour; not just the indignant bluster of the Diabelli Variations, but a purely musical wit unmatched since Haydn. The balance of heterogeneity and inner harmony is questionable only in the B flat quartet, which suffers from the 'finale problem'. Beethoven himself removed the Great Fugue from this position, publishing it separately (op. 133). This wonderful work remains formidable although parts of it are of Olympian geniality. Its technical difficulty matches its complexity of form and its immense scale; Beethoven accordingly replaced it with a rondo finale, his last work. Opinions will always differ over which finale is better; the fugue, however, like the finale of the Ninth, has enough sections to stand on its own, while the rondo is an appealing resolution of tensions which the fugue somewhat exacerbates. That such questions cannot be finally settled is a measure of the significance Beethoven's last works possess for musicians.

The noble E flat and deceptively slight F major quartets seem relatively unproblematical. Even the enigma of op. 135 – its 'very difficult question: Must it be?' – is musically resolved by the joyous response – 'It must be!' – which turns the mood over by inverting the theme. The B flat quartet makes a point of the juxtaposition of opposites: the slow movement in D flat is followed by a capricious dance *alla tedesca* in the remotest key, G, then before the finale (fugue or rondo) comes a Romantic cavatina in E flat. The A minor quartet is hardly less wilful, although it keeps to a traditional relation of keys (A minor and major, and F). At its heart is the austere 'Song of thanksgiving of a convalescent', an image of pure counterpoint in a 'Lydian mode' which probably never existed in polyphonic Church music. It is followed by a brash march, then a flood of disordered passion (recitative) is channelled in a sweeping but still melancholy finale.

Superficially, the C sharp minor quartet is the strangest of all, but experiment is banished and contrast of mood and tonality with it. Its overall plan is shown in fig. 3.

Fig. 3   Beethoven's string quartet in C sharp minor, op. 131

	4 Variations (diverse tempi) A major	
3 Short recitative		*6* Short lament G ♯ minor
2 Lyrical Allegro D major	*5* Scherzo Presto E major	
1 Fugue Adagio C♯ minor		*7* Finale Sonata allegro C ♯ minor

The arch form is rendered asymmetrical by the extreme contrast of speed between the outer movements, which however share a motivic idea, and by the changed order of the major-key fast movements and the short movements. At the apex is an extended set of variations which ranges from Adagio to Allegretto; yet this most sectionalized of forms here flows with complete smoothness, in this reflecting the whole quartet, which plays without a break between movements. Even the remotest key-relation, from C sharp minor to D, is smoothed by the anticipation of the note D throughout the fugue, and by an octave figure at its close which becomes the theme of the second movement. An ideal balance is obtained between contrasts which are integrated, and elements of integration – like the main key – presented as contrasts. The design is unique, yet it is no less clear than the conventional four-movement plan whose retention in the major instrumental works of Beethoven's admiring posterity smacks of timidity. Schubert, who had this quartet played to him in his last illness, might have ventured somewhere on this path, which

Mendelssohn quickly abandoned as being alien to his temperament; Schumann cultivated other fields altogether.

Perhaps later composers could justify their use of more conventional plans by the need to control far wilder ideas. Beethoven, for all his rebelliousness, his individuality, and his novelty of forms, must have been quickly understood by the most advanced musical minds as a profoundly orderly composer. His last works employ fragments but are not fragmentary; they are free but never incoherent; despite their far-reaching imagination, they are a summation of earlier musical techniques, Baroque and Classical, sensitive, stormy and stressful but firmly controlled, their eccentricity superficial, their normality as human documents profound.

Select bibliography

Abraham, Gerald (ed.), *The Age of Beethoven* (*New Oxford History of Music* VIII) (Oxford and New York, 1982); see especially Winton Dean, 'French Opera', 'Italian Opera', 'German Opera' (Chapters 2, 9 and 10)

Atlas, Allan W., *Music in the Classic Period* (New York, 1985)

Barrington, Daines. See Deutsch, *Mozart*.

Blume, Friedrich, *Classic and Romantic Music* (London and New York, 1970)

Brook, Barry S., 'Sturm und Drang and the Romantic Period in Music', *Studies in Romanticism* 9 (1970), 169

Brown, Clive, *Spohr. A Critical Biography* (Cambridge, 1984)

Brown, Maurice J. E., *Schubert: a Critical Biography* (London, 1958)

Budden, Julian, *The Operas of Verdi* I (London, 1973); see 'Verdi and the World of the *Primo Ottocento*' (Chapter 1)

Burney, Charles, *A General History of Music* IV (London, 1789; new edn ed. F. Mercer, London, 1935)

——, *The Present State of Music in France and Italy* (London, 1771); see Scholes

——, *The Present State of Music in Germany, the Netherlands, and the United Provinces* (London, 1773); see Scholes

Charlton, David, *Grétry and the Growth of Opéra-Comique* (Cambridge, 1986)

Cooper, Martin, *Opéra Comique* (London, 1949)

D'Alembert, Jean le Rond, 'Discours préliminaire' in the *Encyclopédie* (Paris, 1751)

——, 'De la liberté de la musique', in *Mélanges de littérature, d'histoire, et de philosophie* (2nd edn, Paris, 1759)

Dent, Edward J., *The Rise of Romantic Opera* (Cambridge, 1976)

Deutsch, Otto Erich, *Mozart: a Documentary Biography* (London, 1965)

——, *Schubert: a Documentary Biography* (London, 1946)

Dittersdorf, Carl von, *Lebensbeschreibung* (Leipzig, 1801; English trans., 1896)

Einstein, Alfred, *Mozart; his Character, his Work* (New York, 1945; London, 1946)

Fiske, Roger, *English Theatre Music in the Eighteenth Century* (Oxford, 1973)

Framery, Nicolas, and Ginguené, Pierre, *Encyclopédie méthodique* (*Musique* I) (Paris, 1791)

——, *Discours qui a remporté le prix de musique et déclamation* (Paris, 1802)

Geiringer, Karl, *Haydn: a Creative Life in Music* (3rd edn, revised and enlarged, London, 1982)

Goethe, J. W. von, *Wilhelm Meisters Wanderjahre* (1820): see Le Huray and Day

Gotwals, V., *Haydn: two Contemporary Portraits* (trans. of early biographical memoirs by Griesinger (1810) and Dies (1810) (Madison, 1963)

Grimsley, Ronald (ed.), *The Age of Enlightenment* (Pelican Guides to European Literature) (Harmondsworth, 1979)

Hanson, Alice M., *Musical Life in Biedermeier Vienna* (Cambridge, 1985)

Hoffmann, E. T. A., 'Beethoven's Fifth Symphony', see Elliot Forbes (ed.), *Beethoven, Fifth Symphony* (Norton Critical Scores) (New York, 1971)

Holmes, Edward, *A Ramble among the Musicians of Germany* (London, 1828)

Honour, Hugh, *Neo-Classicism* (Style and Civilization) (Harmondsworth, 1968)

——, *Romanticism* (Style and Civilization) (Harmondsworth, 1979)

Howard, Patricia, *Gluck and the Birth of Modern Opera* (London, 1963)

Kermode, Frank, *The Classic* (New York and London, 1975)

Landon, H. C. Robbins, *Beethoven: a Documentary Study* (London and New York, 1975)

——, *Haydn: Chronicle and Works* (five volumes) (London and Bloomington, 1976–80)

——, and Chapman, Roger E. (eds), *Studies in Eighteenth-Century Music* (London, 1970)

Lesure, François (ed.), *Querelle des Gluckistes et des Piccinnistes* (2 vols; vol. 1 includes Marmontel, *Essai*), Paris, 1984

Le Huray, Peter, and Day, James, *Music and Aesthetics in the Eighteenth and Early Nineteenth Centuries* (Cambridge, 1981)

Liebner, Janos, *Mozart on the Stage* (London, 1972)

Lowinsky, Edward E., 'Taste, Style and Ideology in Eighteenth-Century Music', see Wasserman

Marmontel, Jean François, *Essai sur les révolutions de la musique en France* (Paris, 1777); see Lesure

Momigny, Jérome Joseph de, *Encyclopédie méthodique* (*Musique*, II) (Paris, 1818)

Mueller von Asow, H. and E. H. (eds), *The Collected Correspondence and Papers of Christoph Willibald Gluck* (London, 1962)

Newman, William S., 'Emanuel Bach's Autobiography', *The Musical Quarterly* 51 (1965), 363

Pestelli, Giorgio, *The Age of Mozart and Beethoven* (Cambridge, 1984)

Plantinga, Leon, *Clementi: his Life and Music* (London, 1977)

Ratner, Leonard G., *Classic Music: Expression, Form, and Style* (New York, 1979)

Robinson, Michael F., *Naples and Neapolitan Opera* (Oxford, 1972)

Rosen, Charles, *The Classical Style* (London and New York, 1971)

——, *Sonata Forms* (New York, 1980)

Rosselli, John, *The Opera Industry in Italy from Cimarosa to Verdi* (Cambridge, 1984).

Rousseau, Jean-Jacques, *Dictionnaire de musique* (Paris, 1768)

——, *Ecrits sur la musique*, in *Oeuvres complètes* (Paris, 1788–93)

Sadie, Stanley (ed.), *The New Grove Dictionary of Music and Musicians* (London, 1980); see especially Daniel Heartz, 'Classical'; 'Empfindsamkeit', 'Enlightenment', 'Galant', 'Rococo', 'Sturm und Drang'

Schlegel, A. W., *Vorlesung über schöne Literatur und Kunst* (1801): see Le Huray and Day.

Scholes, Percy (ed.), *Dr Burney's Musical Tours in Europe* (2 vols) (Oxford, 1959)

Schopenhauer, A., *Die Welt als Wille und Vorstellung* (1819; actually Dec. 1818): see Le Huray and Day

Solomon, Maynard, *Beethoven* (New York and London, 1978)

Spohr, Louis, *Selbstbiographie* (Kassel and Göttingen, 1860–61; English trans., 1865)

Stendhal (H. M. Beyle), *Vie de Rossini* (Paris, 1824; English trans., 1956)

Strunk, Oliver, *Source Readings in Music History* (New York, 1950)

Thayer, A. W., *Life of Beethoven* (rev. and ed. Elliot Forbes, Princeton, 1964)

Wangermann, Ernst, *The Austrian Achievement* (London, 1973)

Warrack, John, *Carl Maria von Weber* (London, 1968)

—— (ed.), *Carl Maria von Weber: Writings on Music* (Cambridge, 1981)

Wasserman, Earl R., *Aspects of the Eighteenth Century* (Baltimore, 1965)

Webb, Daniel, *Observations on the Correspondence between Poetry and Music* (1769), see Le Huray and Day

Wellesz, Egon, and Sternfeld, F. W. (eds), *The Age of Enlightenment* (*New Oxford History of Music* VII) (Oxford, 1973)

Wolf, Eugene K., *The Symphonies of Johann Stamitz* (Utrecht, 1981)

List of illustrations

Index